"THE REALLY GOOD
GHOST STORIES
HAVE SOME CONNECTION
WITH HISTORY."

—Kathryn Tucker Windham,
American storyteller

Carolrhoda Books
A division of Lerner Publishing Group, Inc.
241 First Avenue North
Minneapolis, MN 55401 USA

For reading levels and more information, look up this title at www.lernerbooks.com.

Main body text set in Brioso Pro 11/16.
Typeface provided by Adobe Systems.

Library of Congress Cataloging-in-Publication Data

Walker, Sally M.
        Ghost walls : the story of a 17th-century colonial homestead/ by Sally M. Walker.
            pages   cm
        Includes bibliographical references and index.
        ISBN 978–0–7613–5408–6 (lib. bdg. : alk. paper)
        ISBN 978–1–4677–4625–0 (eBook)
        1. Saint John's Freehold (Saint Mary's City, Md.)—Juvenile literature. 2. Dwellings—Maryland—Saint Mary's City—Juvenile literature. 3. Maryland—History—Colonial period, ca. 1600–1775—Juvenile literature. I. Title.
        F189.S14W35 2014
        975.2'02—dc23   2013036606

Manufactured in the United States of America
1 – BP – 7/15/14

Sally M. Walker

GHOST WALLS

THE STORY OF A
17th-CENTURY COLONIAL HOMESTEAD

CAROLRHODA BOOKS • MINNEAPOLIS

Prologue

More than one kind of ghost haunts a place called St. John's, near St. Mary's City, Maryland.

In 1656 a man called Antonio lay on the ground in front of the house at St. John's and refused to stand. Simon Overzee, the owner of St. John's, cut sticks from a nearby pear tree, strode to Antonio, and "whipd' him upon his bare back." Antonio remained motionless. When a servant tried to help Antonio, Overzee, still holding the knife he had used to cut the stick, "threatened . . . to runne his knife in him [the servant]," if he interfered.

Overzee ordered another servant to heat a small shovel and bring some lard. He melted the lard in the hot shovel and poured it on Antonio's back. Antonio stood but still refused to obey Overzee's commands.

On Overzee's order, an enslaved American Indian tied Antonio to a ladder that was leaning against the front wall of St. John's house. Antonio stood, his arms tied above his head, in the triangle of space created by the leaning ladder and the front wall of St. John's house.

Fifteen minutes later, Overzee and his wife left the house, leaving Antonio tied to the ladder. Fearing punishment from Overzee, no one released him. As the minutes passed, Antonio's legs grew weaker. His knees buckled; his body sagged. Yet his body remained upright, held so by the ropes that lashed his wrists to the ladder. Increasingly, the weight of his hanging body squeezed his lungs tight and then tighter. At first, breathing was difficult; soon he couldn't breathe at all. Within three hours, Antonio suffocated to death.

The stick Overzee used to beat Antonio decayed long ago. Most likely the ladder and rope did too. Antonio's body has never been found. All physical traces of Antonio's life have vanished. But a seventeenth-century official wrote about what had happened. If it hadn't been for those written documents—the historical record—we wouldn't know Antonio had ever existed, let alone how brutally he had been treated. He would have become one of St. John's forgotten ghosts.

Almost twenty years earlier, a carpenter worked near the spot where Antonio later died. Unlike Antonio, an enslaved African, the carpenter chose to immigrate to Maryland and he was paid for his work at St. John's. One of his jobs was sawing planks. He stood inside a pit and used a pit saw with another carpenter who stood on a platform outside the pit. A thick log, supported by the platform, lay with one end hanging over the edge of the pit. The men placed the teeth of their two-handled saw against the cut end of the log. Then, working as a team, the two carpenters pulled the saw up and down cutting the planks needed to build the house. With every downward and upward cut, sawdust rained on the carpenter standing in the pit.

The historical record carries no description, or even mention, of this pit. Yet we know it existed, because archaeologists found and excavated it. The pit is part of St. John's archaeological record. Both the pit and the sawdust it contained became ghosts of a different kind, not of a person but of the work done by colonial carpenters, whose craft and creation were still there in spirit.

For seventy-five years, the walls of St. John's house sheltered many men, women, and children. They absorbed nearly a century's worth of sweat, laughter, tears, and so much more. People sought justice at St. John's. The first man of African ancestry who cast a vote on American soil did so inside its walls. They surrounded the first English woman in America when she requested that same opportunity. St. John's walls knew luxury, but they knew lean times too. They stood firm during pledges made between Englishmen and Native Americans. In their final years, they echoed with requests for a hot evening meal and a bed for the night. St. John's house fell into ruin more than two hundred years ago, its walls becoming yet another kind of ghost. However, historians and archaeologists felt certain that if information from the historical and archaeological records were combined, St. John's house could tell hundreds of stories. But as everyone knows, walls—especially ghost walls—can't talk.

Or can they?

HOUSE HUNTING

By the mid-1700s, St. John's house was no more than rubble buried by soil and overgrown with shrubs and trees. No plans or sketches of the once-grand house built in 1638 have ever been discovered. Yet old stories told about St. Mary's City often mentioned it. Eventually, St. John's house became an enigma. Curious historians scoured documents in the historical record, and eventually the careful reading of thousands of time-yellowed papers paid off. Researchers learned that the house had been a gathering place for influential men at a formative time in America's history—the site of significant events. They found very specific descriptions of some of those events, the harrowing tale of Antonio's brutal death among them. But with respect to the house's appearance, they found little more than tantalizing snippets mentioned in passing during court testimonies. Those who had hoped to find precise descriptions of the house were out of luck.

That's when archaeologists joined the search. They specialize in finding and interpreting physical evidence of past peoples and places. In 1962 Henry Chandlee Forman, an architectural historian who had studied the archaeology of other sites at St. Mary's City, began his own hunt for St. John's house. Armed with knowledge from the historical record, plus the stories of area residents, Forman crisscrossed through the woods where the house once stood. He pushed aside shrubs and brushed away dead leaves until he found a concentration of seventeenth-century bricks and pieces of roofing tiles—small whispers of the long-lost house. In that area, he excavated a series of test trenches that eventually exposed the outline of a cellar. At that point, Forman had a partial picture of the size and floor plan of St. John's house. It was a good foundation for further study.

The next excavations began in 1972 under the leadership of archaeologist Garry Wheeler Stone. Before digging, Stone's crew established a system of perpendicular lines called a grid. Like a piece of graph paper, the lines of a grid create squares across an archaeological site. Each square received its own identifying number. Once the soil, artifacts, and features—evidence of things such as a fireplace or a wall—have been removed from a site, they can never be replaced exactly as they were originally. Yet reinterpreting evidence and revising old theories in the light of new discoveries are important parts of the scientific process. Bearing this in mind, archaeologists always measure and map the exact location of everything they find to ensure that future archaeologists will know how the site had appeared before and during excavation. Stone's team wrote notes, took photographs, and drew numerous diagrams.

As excavations continued, the crew also paid close attention to the stratigraphy. Stratigraphy is a branch of geology that studies rock and soil layers. The central principle of stratigraphy is simple: unless natural or man-made processes—mountain-building or agriculture, for example—have disturbed a sequence of soil layers, the deepest layer is always the oldest one and layers

Sometimes an archaeologist inadvertently becomes part of a dig. Henry Chandlee Forman left this trowel behind during his excavations in 1962. Garry Wheeler Stone's crew found it a decade later during their dig.

Garry Stone and his assistants set up a surveyor's transit (a tool to measure horizontal and vertical angles) as they prepared to establish a grid of lines on the site of St. John's house.

Archaeologists meticulously noted the stratigraphy of the site. Changes in the soil's color provided information about activities that occurred on the site and about the building's construction.

get younger the closer they are to the surface. On a dig, stratigraphy enables archaeologists to interpret the arrangement of soil layers and the features and artifacts found within them into a timeline. The stratigraphy at St. John's could tell Stone a lot about how the house first appeared and how it changed during its seventy-five-year occupation.

When Stone's crew began work, inches-deep soil buried the foundation; for decades, farmers had plowed the yard and the fields that surrounded it. Churning blades scrambled the layers in the uppermost 6 to 8 inches (15 to 20 centimeters). Knowing they wouldn't be digging into undisturbed layers, the crew shoveled this soil into buckets and screened it.

With the plowed soil removed, the archaeologists excavated the undisturbed layers beneath at a much slower pace, trading their shovels for trowels, brushes, and dental picks. As they excavated, the crew saw bricks and cobblestones without any difficulty. They recognized these items were important features of St. John's house, but further study was often necessary before the archaeologists could identify when the feature had become part of the house. As before, they screened the excavated soil for artifacts, occasionally using fine-meshed window screening. In this way,

As separate excavation trenches connected with one another, they revealed St. John's cobblestone foundation and brick chimneys.

Men and women held clothing together with drawstrings and small metal hooks like this one (above) found while crew members screened the soil at St. John's (left).

they collected items as tiny as a clothing hook. Other discoveries were even harder to see. Sometimes, a stain in the soil is the only remaining whisper of a colonial feature—a wooden post that was once part of a wall, for example. So, in addition to looking for items on their screens, the archaeologists carefully watched for subtle changes in soil color and texture.

Excavations conducted from 1972 to 1976 uncovered many features and hundreds of thousands of artifacts. One broken artifact particularly captured the archaeologists' imaginations. The object, made from white clay, was the back of a small head carved with curls of hair. "We didn't know what it was," said Silas Hurry, the curator of collections and the director of the Archaeological Laboratory at St. Mary's City. "We classified it as a possible doll part or a decoration made from white clay." The artifact was placed in a storage cabinet. During the later 1970s and the 1980s, various specialists examined the curious artifact, but none of them could identify it. And everyone who saw it wondered what the face had looked like.

For decades, historians and many types of scientists collected pieces of the St. John's house puzzle. Meanwhile, historians searched libraries, archives, and

Left: *The discovery of the back portion of a small head made of white clay left the entire team wondering what the unusual artifact might have been.*

Right: *To the untrained eye, these dark circles of soil don't mean anything. But an archaeologist recognizes them as evidence of a building.*

collections in America and England for more information. Their discoveries aided the archaeologists as they revealed the features, soil stains, and artifacts that were all that remained of St. John's house. Biologists and geologists offered insight into the fauna, the flora, and the rock materials that colonial workers had used. The combined knowledge of all of these investigators not only told the story of people who worked hard, but it gave the investigators the information they needed to make ghost walls materialize.

"DWELL HERE, LIVE PLENTIFULLY AND BE RICH"

T he solid walls of St. John's house were built with wood, nails, and the hopes and dreams of a man named John Lewger. On November 28, 1637, John Lewger, his wife, Anne, and their son disembarked from the *Unity* when it anchored near St. Mary's City. On legs still wobbly from months of sea travel, the Lewgers and their seven servants walked the short distance to the fort. Despite being Maryland's first provincial secretary, an important governmental job, John and his family would live in one of the small, crude wooden cottages inside the fort's palisade walls until John built a new home. Living in colonial Maryland was risky, dangerous even. But John believed the colony's rich soil and bountiful forests offered a rewarding future. Equally important, Maryland's government promised the Lewgers a freedom they were denied in England, a freedom that began as the daring dream of a man named George Calvert.

As a boy, George Calvert and his family were persecuted because they were Roman Catholic. England's persecution of Catholics began long before George's birth in 1579. In 1534 King Henry VIII severed ties with the Catholic Church and established the Church of England as England's official church. In time, the Church of England became more aligned with the Protestant branch of Christianity. In Calvert's day, Catholics could not worship publicly, could not attend English universities, and could not hold a job in the government. English Protestants didn't believe Catholics could be equally loyal to their religious leader, the pope, and to England. Some Protestants suspected Catholics of treachery, even treason. Government authorities forced many Catholics, George's father among them, to worship in the Church of England. To avoid persecution and imprisonment, George's father converted to the Church of England. When George was twelve years old, government authorities ordered him sent away from his home to be educated by a Protestant tutor. When he was a teen, George formally joined the Church of England.

George Calvert (left) bought his country estate in North Yorkshire in 1619. He built Kiplin Hall (right) during the early 1620s as his family's country retreat and hunting lodge. As a young man, Roman Catholic George Calvert was subjected to religious persecution. As an adult, he planned to establish a colony where a person's religion could not bar him from educational opportunities and certain careers.

As the years passed, George Calvert became powerful and wealthy. He served as one of England's two secretaries of state, and he owned land in England and in a colony in Newfoundland, in America. He and his wife had ten children, including his son and heir, Cecil. George was on top of the world.

Then it all unraveled. His wife died in childbirth. In 1625 George lost the political favor of Parliament, England's legislative body. He resigned from his position as secretary of state. Immediately afterward, he converted back to Catholicism. Despite his political misfortune, he remained in the good graces of the king, who granted George land in Ireland and gave him the title of Lord Baltimore.

By 1628 George moved his family to Newfoundland, in North America, leaving his son Cecil behind to manage the family's business affairs. Unfortunately, the Newfoundland colony failed. George returned to England, where he and Cecil spent the next three years negotiating with King Charles I for a royal charter to establish a colony next to Virginia, where George saw great opportunity. They succeeded. George's colony would be named the Province of Maryland, in honor of the king's Catholic wife, Queen Henrietta Maria.

Cecil Calvert enticed additional colonists to Maryland with a pamphlet—including this map—that extolled the colony as a land of opportunity and riches.

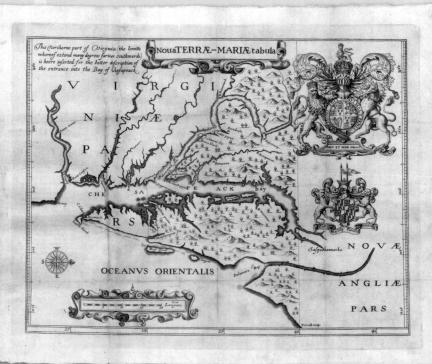

The charter's terms named George and his heirs the colony's lord proprietors. As such, he had the authority to create laws for Maryland. George intended to use this power in an unprecedented way: to separate religion and politics.

George died in 1632, just weeks before the charter was signed. Twenty-six-year-old Cecil Calvert received the charter in his father's stead, becoming Maryland's first lord proprietor, as well as the second Lord Baltimore. Following his father's wishes, Cecil instituted a policy called liberty of conscience. In Maryland, Christians could worship

Although Cecil Calvert (above), George's heir, lived to the age of seventy, he was only twenty-six when he became Maryland's lord proprietor. Cecil married Anne Arundell. The ceiling in one of the rooms of their home is sculpted with images of two ships, which historians believe represent the Ark and the Dove.

The Maryland Dove is a re-creation of the seventeenth-century trading vessels that carried the supplies to Lord Baltimore's new American colony called Maryland.

as they pleased without penalty or discrimination. Freedom of this kind was unheard of in seventeenth-century England.

Preparations for the move to Maryland took more than a year. But finally, in November 1633, two ships, the *Ark* and the *Dove*, departed from England. Most of the 140 passengers on board the *Ark* were Protestants, but 17 were wealthy Catholic gentlemen and 3 were Catholic priests.

Cecil appointed his brother Leonard governor of the province. Aware that tension between Catholics and Protestants might arise during the long journey, Cecil ordered Leonard "to preserve unity & peace amongst all the passengers on

While some colonists remained on the Ark, others moved into Yaocomaco dwellings, similar to this re-creation (left), made with reeds. To build the fort's four 360-foot (110-meter) walls, the men placed wooden logs upright and side by side, into the ground (below). This type of wall is called a palisade wall. The actual walls would have been 8 to 10 feet (3 m) high, several feet higher than this modern reconstruction.

Eight cannons guarded Fort St. Mary from feared attacks by American Indians or hostile Virginians. This cannon, along with several others, was found in the St. Mary's River in 1823 and raised. The style dates to manufacturing processes used in the first half of the seventeenth century. For this reason, archaeologists conclude that it was on the Ark and likely within Fort St. Mary.

Shipp-board, and that the [Catholics] suffer no scandall nor offence to be given to any of the Protestants" that they might later complain about.

In March 1634, the *Ark* and the *Dove* landed at St. Clement's Island, in the Potomac River. Before proceeding farther, Leonard traveled upriver and met with the "Emperour" of the Piscataway Indians. The two "settled a firme peace" and Leonard obtained "leave . . . to sett downe where we pleased." Meanwhile, his men on St. Clement's Island felled trees, split logs, and readied them for loading onto the *Dove.* Cecil Calvert's instructions made building a fort the colonists' first priority as soon as a permanent settlement site was chosen. Leonard acquired a tract of cleared land along the St. Mary's River from the Yaocomaco Indians, who lived there. The colonists named their new home St. Mary's City. Jamestown, Virginia, a 100-mile (161-kilometer) boat trip away, was the only other English town in the Chesapeake Bay region.

Half of the Yaocomaco departed for summer hunting grounds; those who remained behind shared their village with the colonists. As the men built the fort within "one halfe mile of the river," they even enclosed some of the Yaocomaco's reed dwellings within the fort.

By May the fort was finished. Next, the men built one-story, wooden cottages inside the fort, where the colonists would live for the first few years. (Three years later, the Lewgers moved into one of these cottages.)

Father Andrew White, one of the Catholic priests, fulfilled one of George

Calvert's dreams when he openly preached Catholic masses in one of the vacated Indian dwellings. Even though holding Mass was legally permissible, Cecil Calvert still requested that Catholics not discuss or debate religion with Protestants and that the government "treat the Protestants with as much mildness and favor as Justice will permitt."

While Leonard sent men upriver on the *Dove* to trade English goods for beaver skins, others ventured outside the fort to collect food for the upcoming winter. Yaocomaco planters already grew corn, but the colonists needed their own supply. Yet cleared fields were few and large trees grew in most places. Rather than chopping down fully grown trees, which would have required a lot of labor and consumed a great deal of time, the colonists followed Yaocomaco practices and girdled them. The colonists' fields, studded with the skeletons of girdled trees, were a far cry from England's neatly manicured farmlands. Since they had few cattle and no horses, plowing was not an option.

Girdling is the process of stripping all the bark around a section of a tree's trunk. This prevents nutrients from reaching the leaves. After the leaves withered and fell, the colonists sowed corn seeds between the trunks. Sunlight that shone through the bare branches nourished the growing corn plants.

Throughout the spring and the summer, the colonists tended the corn and gathered stores of nuts and fruit from the forests. And of course they planted tobacco, the crop that everyone hoped would make them rich.

During the next three years, colonists began to build homes outside the fort's walls. George and Cecil Calvert designed Maryland's government as a manorial system, a long-standing English system of property ownership. Under this system, Cecil granted a manor—1,000 acres (405 hectares) of land—to any man who brought five male servants to Maryland. That man became the lord of the manor, with certain governing rights. In turn, each manorial lord paid Cecil an annual quitrent, or sum of money, for his land "to be paid in the Commodities of the Countrey," meaning tobacco or fur. (In comparison, Cecil paid the king only two American Indian arrows each year to own Maryland—more than 12,000 square miles [31,000 sq. km.].) Free laborers, servants, and others lived in dwellings on the manors. The manorial lords were Maryland's powerbrokers; they controlled the province's land, laborers, and trade with England. They answered only to the Calverts. The Calverts believed controlling society in this way was essential while organizing a frontier colony as yet undeveloped by Europeans.

The king required Cecil Calvert to pay him two arrows annually as his quitrent for Maryland. The arrows would have been tipped with a stone point similar to this one.

Colonists established homes and plantations along Maryland's abundant waterways. They transported tobacco and furs to trade ships embarking for England. Living near water speeded the delivery of goods from England. And all the while, Catholics and Protestants lived in relative harmony. Slowly, Marylanders carved their place in America, furthering their own hopes and the Calverts' colonial dream. John Lewger was one of the men who could make the Calverts' plan a reality.

Although the Lewgers didn't know it, when the *Unity* anchored near St. Mary's City, the land that would soon become their home could be seen from the ship's deck. When they disembarked, they became part of George and Cecil Calvert's Maryland dream. They had no idea there would also be nightmares.

John Lewger's life in Maryland would be very different from his life in England. Born in 1601, Lewger was the son of a scrivener, a person who copies or writes documents for a fee. Lewger studied theology at Oxford University's Trinity College, where he and Cecil Calvert became friends.

Initially ordained as a priest in the Church of England, Lewger later returned to Trinity College for further study. While there, a friend persuaded him to study Catholic theology. The more he studied, the more Lewger became convinced that Catholicism was the true religion. By mid-summer of 1635, Lewger left the Church of England and converted to Catholicism. This was a huge step for him; in doing so, he lost all of his sources of income.

Cecil Calvert, who by then had become Lord Baltimore, believed Lewger's abilities could benefit Maryland. He introduced Lewger to Jerome Hawley, one of the Catholic men who had sailed on the *Ark* in 1633. Lewger and Hawley collaborated on a document titled *A Relation of Maryland* for Cecil Calvert. It was essentially a recruiting pamphlet. Hawley's firsthand knowledge of the colony combined with Lewger's vivid text persuaded many people to join Lord Baltimore's Maryland adventure. "The Timber of these parts is very good, and . . . is usefull for building . . . houses, and shippes;. . . . the Chesnuts, and what rootes they find in the woods, doe feede the Swine very fat." The pamphlet recommended the best time of year to arrive and listed the supplies a colonist needed to bring to ensure his or her survival.

Lewger's integrity and organizational skills continued to impress Cecil. On April 15, 1637, he hired Lewger as Maryland's provincial secretary. He would also serve as a counselor, collect all payments due to Lord Baltimore, and act as the colony's surveyor general. When John Lewger stepped ashore at St. Mary's City, he was one of Maryland's most important officials. In acknowledgment of this, Cecil granted Lewger a freehold of 200 acres (81 hectares) of townland, outright, as a special warrant.

After looking at several properties, Lewger chose land that was a fifteen-minute walk from the fort. In honor of his patron saint, Lewger named the property St. John's. With fertile soil, easy access to the harbor via Mill Pond (near St. John's front yard) and a freshwater spring, the property perfectly met the Lewgers' needs.

The Lewgers' property became known as St. John's freehold. Prior to English colonization, Native Americans used the area seasonally for temporary lodging and crops.

THE HOUSE THAT JOHN BUILT

Building St. John's house, a grand home by colonial Maryland standards, was a major undertaking. "The preparation and building of St. John's took at least a year and perhaps fourteen to fifteen months total time. Just the preparation of materials was a major task," said archaeologist Henry Miller, the director of research at Historic St. Mary's City.

As most people do when building a new home, John Lewger hired laborers to do the actual construction. The Lewgers' servants would also have aided the hired men. The Lewgers brought seven indentured servants with them from England. These people—three men, three women, and a boy—each signed (or made his or her mark if unable to write) a legal document, called an indenture, binding them to John Lewger. As their master, Lewger paid the cost of their transportation to America and, during the term of the contract, provided them room and board in Maryland. In exchange, they agreed to work for Lewger for a specific length of time, usually four to seven years. Without asking permission, Lewger could sell a servant's indenture to a third party. In 1638, when he was ready to establish his plantation, John Lewger purchased the indentures of seven additional men, including a carpenter, a gardener, and a tailor.

Arriving as a family unit, as the Lewgers had, was unusual for the time period. Before 1650 most of the immigrants to Maryland were unmarried indentured servants, who lived in their master's house or in nearby servants' quarters. Most were between seventeen and twenty-eight years old. Some, including twelve-year-old Robert Serle, who came with the Lewgers, were younger. Some servants had trades, such as masonry or carpentry, but many were farm laborers or untrained workers. During Maryland's first year as a colony, men outnumbered women six to one.

John Lewger quickly added more acres to his Maryland land holdings. He received 50 acres (20 hectares) for each of the seven indentured servants he transported to Maryland, as did all English landowners who brought servants. (He also received 50 acres [20 hectares] for each member of his own family.) But no servants received their reward until after they completed their indenture. Then Lewger would be required to give a servant his or her freedom dues: an axe, two farm tools (a hoe, for example), three barrels of corn, and a new suit of clothes. At that time, the provincial government gave the free person the right to buy 50 acres of land after he or she paid certain fees.

There were no guarantees that a servant would live long enough to collect his or her freedom dues. Despite the risk of death and the certainty of hard work, people indentured themselves for the chance of a better life, and masters purchased the indentures because they needed the labor.

In 1638 everyone who lived at St. Mary's City knew about the Lewgers' new house. Construction sounds, sights, and smells filled the air. Laborers, eyes ever alert for venomous copperheads and poison ivy, called to one another as they cleared away shrubs and herbaceous plants such as ragweed, goldenrod, and goosefoot. Wood chips flew as axe blades chunked into tree trunks. Branches snapped as oak and chestnut trees toppled and crashed to the ground. Along the river, men slipped in the mud as they collected cobbles that had eroded from the riverbank. A boat floated tools and materials across Mill Pond. Sometimes, clouds of smoke wafted from the construction site. Iron spades, picks, shovels, and hoes clanked as workers dug a rectangular trench for the house's foundation. Two sides of the rectangle were 52 feet (16 m) long; the other two sides were 20.5 feet (6 m) long. Cobblestones clacked together as the laborers stacked them in the foundation trench.

St. John's durable stone foundation was a standout feature at St. Mary's City. The frames of most Maryland houses were supported by or on top of the exposed ends of wooden posts buried upright in the ground. Termites, the scourge of Chesapeake builders, soon chewed them, which weakened the building's integrity. John Lewger wanted his house to last, so he had it built on a stone foundation.

The soil at St. John's also held another interesting feature: a cellar, unique because it was very large and its walls had been lined with stone. The historical record doesn't mention a cellar, but excavation and stratigraphy revealed that

The builders finished the cellar's first floor and walls with fire. The red-colored layer of soil at the base of the brick wall was caused when the clay in the original earthen floor and walls was fire-hardened. Stratigraphy showed that the brick wall was added during a later remodeling project.

there was one beneath part of the house and that it had been dug at the same time or shortly before the foundation trench. Furthermore, there was evidence that a bonfire had been lit within the cellar's earthen walls. Silas Hurry noted that "fire reddened earth was visible in the cellar. The clay in the soil had been burned to almost brick color." St. John's soil contains a lot of clay particles. Heat from the flames strengthened the molecular bonds between the clay particles, hardening the earthen floor and walls.

After finishing the foundation and the cellar, Lewger's men dug a number of narrow parallel trenches within the foundation's outline. These trenches, called slot trenches, would hold the floor joists for the two rooms on the house's first floor. As with the cellar, the soil told the story. The joists that supported St. John's floor had decomposed more than two hundred years before archaeologists excavated the site. Yet the decayed joists left clear evidence of their presence as parallel lines of soil stains.

While some men dug trenches, others worked elsewhere. Carpenters Andrew Baker, Francis Gray, and Philip West (who was the Lewgers' nearest neighbor) hewed the rough trunks of white oak and chestnut trees into posts, beams and joists, sills, and clapboards that would be needed to frame and finish the house.

To frame the house, the carpenters first capped the cobblestone foundation with squared timbers set lengthwise. These timbers formed the sill that would anchor the house frame. "There was nothing but gravity holding the house on the cobblestones. Unless there was a tornado, the weight of the house was sufficient to keep it firmly in place," said Henry Miller.

Carpenters hoisted a series of wooden frames into place along the length of the sill, creating a skeletal frame for the house. The finished frame revealed a one-and-a-half-story house that probably had two dormers, one near each end of the house, to provide light for the upper floor. At this time, they also built a stairway, located halfway along the north wall, and installed the frames for windows and doors.

But for a short time, death silenced the sound of hammers at St. John's. Documents tell us that death preyed heavily on Maryland's colonists. Malaria and dysentery killed many within the first six months of their arrival. Many who survived this "seasoning time," as the colonists called it, died in the next

The carpenters chiseled square holes called mortises along the length of the sill. Then the men hoisted preassembled bents into place at each mortise. A bent is a frame made of two upright wall posts connected together at the top with a beam. Each wall post had a squared tab called a tenon at its base. The carpenters snugged the tenon of each wall post into the appropriate mortise in the sill. A wooden peg driven into a hole in the connected timbers further secured each joint.

Additional timbers, each with its own mortise and tenon, linked the bents together at the ceiling, where the first story and the upper half-story met. St. John's was one-and-a-half-stories tall. (The first floor ceiling height of homes of this period was 6 to 6.5 feet [0.8 to 2 m]. Most modern homes have ceilings 8 feet [2.4 m] or higher.) Wall studs placed between the bents added more strength to the frame.

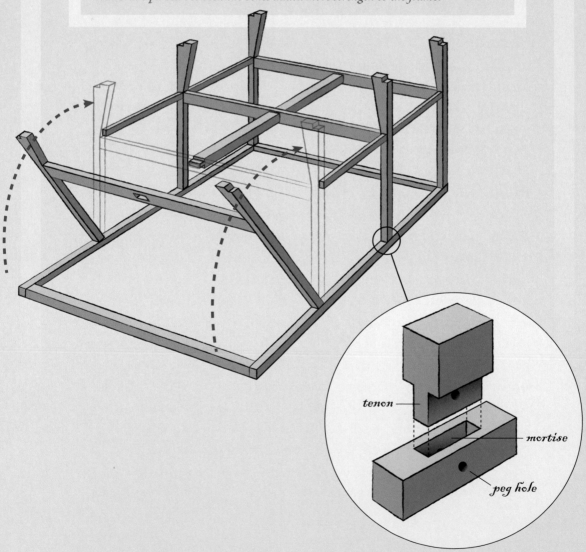

tenon

mortise

peg hole

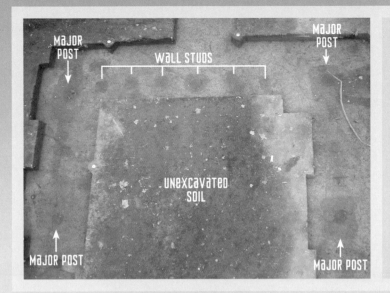

MAJOR POST
MAJOR POST
WALL STUDS
UNEXCAVATED SOIL
MAJOR POST
MAJOR POST

Years of excavation experience, knowledge of seventeenth-century constructions techniques, and comparison with still-existing seventeenth-century structures helped archaeologists interpret the soil stains and how they related to the home's construction.

few years, their health weakened by changes in diet, in climate, and from hard labor. Most men died before the age of fifty. Women lived even shorter lives, partly due to the risks of childbearing. And one-fourth of all the babies born in early colonial Maryland died before their first birthday. It isn't surprising, then, that death touched St. John's house even as its walls were being raised. When historians scoured Maryland's archives for information about the house, they discovered that carpenter Andrew Baker had died August 20, 1638, just months after construction began. There was no mention of what killed him. But one of John Lewger's duties was to list a deceased person's belongings so they could be sold to pay off outstanding debts. Lewger's list is part of the historical record. Baker had owned very few items beyond the carpenter's tools he'd used at St. John's.

While carpenters nailed the wooden frame, other men built a brick chimney with two fireplaces. The cost of importing bricks from England would have been an unthinkable extravagance for even the wealthiest Marylander. Fortunately, Lewger's workers could make bricks from the clay in St. John's soil. "In fact, they might have used some of the soil removed when they dug out the cellar," Miller theorized.

Workers would have mixed water with the clay until it formed a thick, pliable paste. They packed the clay into wooden molds and allowed the bricks to dry in the sun. Finally, they fired the bricks in a temporary kiln called a clamp.

"We found a small brick clamp about 300 feet [91 m] from the house, and it might have been the one used to make the chimney bricks," Miller added.

The bricks extended at least as high as the top of the two back-to-back fireplaces and maybe as high as the ceiling. The rest of the chimneystack was made of wattle and daub. Wattle is a lattice created by interweaving strips of wood. The spaces in the wattle are filled and covered with daub, a sticky mixture of soil, sand, clay, water, straw, and sometimes animal dung. English builders regularly constructed wattle and daub chimneys, which can last for years if repaired annually. "Back in the 1970s, I visited the last standing wattle and daub chimney in the Chesapeake,"

The back-to-back fireplaces in the home's central chimney heated the parlor and the kitchen. Heat rising in the chimney warmed the chambers in the upper half-story.

Three hundred years before Henry Chandlee Forman lost his trowel, a seventeenth-century mason dropped this trowel (above). Stone's crew was thrilled to find it.

stated Miller. "The owner said it worked fine, but the problem was that after each winter and spring rains, you had to re-daub the portions damaged by the weather."

Rethinking and reinterpreting theories in the light of new knowledge is an important part of the scientific process. Archaeologists were puzzled by the small amount of flat roof tiles they found at St. John's. Hearing the present-day homeowner's wattle and daub woes led Miller to a hypothesis about the tiles found at St. John's. "There were not enough roof tiles to cover a building, but the amount would have been sufficient to clad the exposed sections of the chimney." If the uppermost reaches of St. John's chimney had been clad in this way, it would have fared better against inclement weather than uncovered wattle and daub.

By the time St. John's wooden frame and brick chimney were completed, the Lewgers had a good idea of their home's size and appearance. But they didn't have a weather-snug home until the carpenters had nailed clapboards to the roof and the outside of the walls. In comparison to some of the carpentry chores at St. John's, the carpenters found riving (splitting) the clapboards surprisingly easy. "The reason they did is because the wood available at St. John's was so high quality. A skilled worker could have peeled off the clapboards from logs like cutting butter," explained Miller. This is more than speculation on Miller's part. To understand the complexities of colonial building, modern-day carpenters at Historic St. Mary's City built a plantation house using seventeenth-century tools and techniques. "When we were building the house, our crew had one log of very high quality. It was fine-grained, with no knots. They produced great clapboards from it in one-fourth the time it took with less fine timbers."

With the outside of the house nearly complete, the men undertook jobs that would complete the interior of the home. St. John's had several features most colonial Marylanders considered luxuries: plaster walls, wood floors, and glass windows. At the time Lewger built St. John's, the historical record documents only two other houses in St. Mary's City with some of these extras.

Plaster is made with caustic calcium oxide, commonly called quicklime. Making plaster from scratch, as colonial workers did, was a time-consuming chore. First, they collected oyster shells. Next, they burned the shells in an open-air fire on top of a platform made of logs. Burning chemically converted the calcium in the shells into quicklime.

When the shells were completely burned, the men shoveled them into wooden tubs, crushed them, and then sieved them to remove large pieces. Before the next step—adding water—the workers probably covered their hands and arms. Adding water to quicklime causes a chemical reaction that raises the temperature of the mixture to the boiling point. This process is not to be taken lightly. The mixture becomes so hot and so caustic that it can severely burn, even completely destroy, flesh. After stirring the mixture thoroughly, the men poured it into a storage pit in the ground. They let the mixture age in the pit until it was the proper consistency for use, which could take as long as several months or even years. When it was ready, the workers carried the plaster into St. John's house and troweled it onto the lath, narrow strips of split wood fastened in place between the wall's studs. The plasterer swiped the plaster's surface with the straight edge of his trowel to give the wall a smooth finish.

Although the historical record doesn't mention St. John's plaster walls, evidence found by the archaeologists proved the walls' existence and that laborers had done the necessary work. During their excavations, Stone's crew found partially burned oyster shells in an area not associated with cooking and chunks of plaster that contained the "keys" or imprint of the lath on one side.

Wet plaster oozed between the wall laths when it was applied, creating the center ridgeline in this piece of plaster. The striated surfaces on either side of the ridgeline are imprints of the flat lath.

Sawdust filled the hair and clothes of the carpenter who had the unlucky job of working in the saw pit (top). Crew member Wesley Willoughby (left) scrapes the wall of this cross-sectioned feature. It is the pit used by the carpenters at St. John's when they were sawing planks. The dark organic layer along the bottom of the pit (detail above) was created when the sawdust decomposed the lighter colored, much thicker layer above is backfill.

With the surrounding soil brushed away, the crew could easily see the line of floorboard nails, iron-clad proof that St. John's house had wooden floors.

Adding a wood floor—another of St. John's luxury features not mentioned in the historical record—was another time-consuming task. Like the floor joists, the boards of St. John's floor had decomposed more than two hundred years before archaeologists excavated the site. But archaeological evidence conclusively proved the presence of wood floors: a paired line of rusty nails, pounded by the St. John's carpenters through the floorboard and into the joist beneath, still stood upright within the stains, held in place by the surrounding soil.

Every layer of soil or stain that the archaeologists explored told a small story about the house. Slowly, its ghost walls were materializing.

Almost all of St. Mary's City's homes had wooden

shutters that hinged or slid closed. If an open window had any other covering, it would have been oiled cloth or paper. At that time in Maryland, no one was making glass windowpanes. And the historical record is mute on St. John's and its luxurious glass windows. However, archaeologists at St. John's found window glass in the layers of soil associated with the house. But knowing

Diamond-shaped quarrels were typical in seventeenth-century windows. The horizontal bars of wood add support for the lead strips and quarrels, which are flexible despite being soldered.

exactly what kind of windows the carpenters had installed required special knowledge. Excavators found small strips and bits of lead. Henry Miller knew seventeenth-century glassmakers could not make large panes of glass, like those in windows today. Instead, glazers produced smaller glass sheets that were cut into rectangular or diamond-shaped panes of glass called quarrels. Strips of lead held a window's quarrels in place.

Piecing together shards of glass found at St. John's was a laborious task that paid off. That's how the team discovered a previously unknown detail: the house had quarrels more varied than the typical diamond shape.

In the archaeology laboratory at St. Mary's, conservators pieced together some of the glass fragments found at St. John's. They discovered that some of

Colonists used a shot mold like this to shape the round lead shot (inset) used as ammunition for their guns.

the windows had unusually shaped quarrels—another unique touch to the house. They also noticed that some of the lead strips were impressed with the identifying mark of their maker. (Window makers at that time were required to mark their leads.) But the lead strips the archaeologists found had been made by a man who had worked in the 1660s. This did not change the archaeologists' belief that the Lewgers had glass windows. The absence of earlier lead strips is easily explained. Lead was too valuable to waste, so the colonists recycled it. When a window was remodeled or repaired, the old lead strips were removed and melted. The melted lead was then molded into lead shot for the colonists' guns. While it's possible the recycled lead might have been used to make pewter, a metal often used to make plates and spoons, Miller doesn't think it's likely. "The fragments of lead spatter and trimming evidence from shot casting indicates that lead in Maryland was mostly used for making lead shot of various sizes."

The carpenters installed fancy hinges, imported from England, on the doors at St. John's (left). A similar hinge (right) holds a door in Cecil and Anne Arundell Calvert's home in England.

All the windows plus hardware such as door hinges and locks that were used to finish the St. John's house came from England. Although the historical record does not contain a list of items John Lewger brought with him on the *Unity*, their presence proves that he either brought them with him or arranged to have them shipped shortly after his arrival in Maryland. As had the earlier discoveries of cobbles, bricks, plaster, and floor nails, finding the quarrels, hinges, and locks helped rebuild St. John's ghost walls.

Inside the House

A visitor who walked up the path from Mill Pond to St. John's would have been impressed by the house's outer appearance. But the inside of the house—Anne Lewger's domain—was equally impressive. The historical record offered no information about the Lewgers' floor plan. Archaeological excavations supplied all the evidence.

Visitors entered the Lewgers' new home through the front door, into a small entry area called a lobby. "St. John's was a Lobby Entry House," explained Miller. "Having a lobby offered several advantages. It helped keep cold air out of the living spaces. If John and Anne were busy and weather conditions were bad, the lobby served as a holding area for visitors. It was a place where visitors could wipe their feet before entering the actual living spaces." One side of the chimney acted as the lobby's back wall. St. John's massive chimney divided the first floor into two rooms: the parlor at the east end of the house and the kitchen, then called a hall, at the west. From the lobby, visitors entered into the living spaces via two doors, one on each side of the lobby.

The door to the right led to the parlor. Anne and John's parlor had two

When all the construction was finished, the Lewgers had a fine one-and-a-half-story home.

Upholstered furniture was a real luxury in seventeenth-century Maryland. These upholstery tacks found at St. John's are proof that the furniture there was of a high quality.

primary uses: first as the sitting room and second as their bedroom. John also used the parlor for assembly and council meetings and for provincial court sessions. (The assembly was the colony's legislature.) At almost 24 feet (7 m) long and 20 feet (6 m) wide, when it was built St. John's parlor was the largest meeting room in St. Mary's City. A door at the east end of the room led directly outside, making it easy for governmental visitors to enter the parlor without disturbing the rest of the household.

From lists of furnishings that other wealthy St. Mary's residents owned, historians know how the Lewgers probably furnished their parlor. Almost everything in the room came from England. The furnishings would have included items such as a chest, a cupboard, stools, chairs, John's desk, and one or two tables draped with Turkish carpets. In the 1600s, expensive carpets lay on tabletops, not on the floor. A storage closet was to the right of the fireplace. Maryland colonists had little personal or private space, so John and Anne's bedstead completed the parlor's furniture suite. They most likely slept in a four-poster bed hung with curtains that could be drawn for privacy. Given the family's high status, the bed may have had a feather mattress. If so, it would have been the only one in the house. Colonial children did not have their own bedrooms. Young John slept in a corner of the parlor and perhaps in an upstairs chamber when he grew older. Cicely and Anne, the Lewgers' daughters who were born in the years after the family arrived in Maryland, first slept alongside Anne and John's bed, perhaps in a cradle and, later, as toddlers, moved to a mattress placed in the parlor at night.

If visitors chose to exit the lobby via the door on the left, they would have found themselves amidst a flurry of activity in Anne's kitchen, also called the hall. But Anne Lewger and her servants were not the first people to have used that area as a kitchen. Archaeologists who listened for the Lewgers' ghostly whispers occasionally heard ghosts from ancient times. Scarcely 4 feet (1 m) from Anne's 1638 fireplace, archaeologists discovered the remains of an even older hearth. Clearing only the top of the feature, the archaeologists revealed fire-cracked rock. Fire-cracked rock is evidence of a cooking method that predates the use of pottery. Native peoples heated fist-sized rocks in a fire and then dropped the hot rocks into a cooking pit lined with hide and filled with water. The hot rocks heated the water and cooked whatever food had been added to the pit. A rock's structure is weakened when it is repeatedly heated and then plunged into cold water. Eventually, the rock fractures. Archaeologists are trained to recognize rocks broken by this process.

Long before the seventeenth century, many Chesapeake Indian groups lived in the region. "On the St. John's site, we have good evidence—spear points and pottery, for example—of Chesapeake Indian habitation, off and on, over a period of thousands of years. This is perhaps due to the presence of the reliable freshwater spring that also attracted Lewger. But the materials we found suggest short campsites rather than a major village occupied for a long

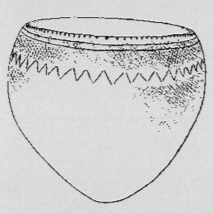

The impressions on these pieces of a type of Native American pottery, known as Popes Creek pottery, were made by pressing a net into the surface of the wet clay. Popes Creek pottery dates from 500 BCE to 300 CE. By piecing together fragments from many Popes Creek vessels, archaeologists have learned that these pots had conical bases. The presence of Popes Creek pottery and the ancient hearth attest to native peoples having utilized the St. John's site for a very long time.

period," Miller explained. "Time, roots, and insects have leached away any charcoal that remained and blurred the edges of the pit. This suggests that it is of considerable age. Several thousand years is a good bet. Clearly these people had used stones to heat water. That would not have been necessary if they had pots—and the earliest American Indian pottery in this area is about three thousand years old. So a working hypothesis is that the cook pit is pre-pottery in date." Rather than excavate the feature, which would destroy it, the archaeologists left it intact for future investigators, who might have new exploratory methods.

Turning their attention from the ancient hearth, the archaeologists focused on the room in which Anne and her servants prepared food and cooked meals.

No documents mention that Anne had a dairy, but Garry Stone's crew excavated a cellar-like addition, 3.5 feet (1 m) by 6 feet (1.8 m), that perfectly fit the needs of such a room. It's easy to imagine why Anne would have wanted a dairy. In the first year or so in her new house, Anne must have stored milk, cream, butter, and cheese in the cool cellar beneath the parlor. However, leaving the kitchen and walking outside to the cellar door at the other end of the house wasted time. Traipsing back and forth through the parlor and then outside and down into the cellar was inconvenient too, especially when the worker was carrying heavy milk pails or large ceramic milk pans that might spill. By about 1640, Anne could easily have decided renovation was in order.

Like a shed, the dairy extended from the rear wall of the house, its floor 4 feet (1 m) belowground. Entering the room through a door in the kitchen, Anne Lewger stepped down five steep stairs to the cobblestone floor. Because the dairy's earthen walls are still crisply defined, archaeologists think that the carpenters lined them with wooden planks, which served as insulation.

Some circular soil stains at ground level just outside the perimeter of the dairy's belowground walls baffled the archaeologists. These holes—called postholes—are holes dug to hold wall posts. The soil used to backfill a posthole around the post has been churned, so its color is slightly different from the surrounding soil, which had not been disturbed by digging. The postholes near the dairy were not along the rim of the small earthen cellar. They were uniformly 18 inches (46 cm) away from the rim. When connected with lines, the postholes outlined a shelflike area, like a wide collar, around the rim of the earthen walls. Archaeologists feel certain these postholes held the wall posts for above-the-ground wooden walls for the dairy. For a worker standing inside the dairy, this area would have been slightly above waist height. Henry Miller visualized Anne and the other women working in the room. He ruled out churning butter. The room was so small that the churn would have taken up too much floor space. Then he imagined the women skimming cream from ceramic milk pans and wrapping cheese for storage and realized they would have needed workspace. Suddenly, the 18-inch (0.5 m) collar made sense: its height and depth were perfect for a built-in countertop.

Superimposing the dairy structure on the archaeological excavations (above) helps us see how the wooden frame was supported. The illustration below shows the completed dairy in use.

The dairy offered Anne and her servants plenty of workspace and storage, and the door at the top of the stairs kept the little room cool, preventing milk, cream, and cheese from spoiling.

At the end of a hard day's work, the Lewgers' servants were glad to head upstairs to bed. While one side of the massive brick chimney faced visitors who entered the lobby, the chimney's other side faced the back of the house. There a steep, narrow staircase ascended from the kitchen to the second floor. (The storage closet in the parlor was located under this staircase.) As it had on the first floor, the massive central chimney divided St. John's upper half story into two chambers. The women servants slept in one of the chambers, the men slept in the other.

Most people who lived in St. Mary's City owned two outfits, at most. Since all cloth was imported from England, clothes were expensive. People mended garments until the patches had patches. St. John's house, like all colonial homes, had no clothes closets. People stored their clothes and other belongings in chests or trunks. Several documents in the historical record mention a trunk in the parlor and in an upper chamber at St. John's. These trunks, made with a lock, contained valuable items, such as lace or spices. Carrying very large furniture up St. John's steep, narrow staircase would have been impossible. Yet the documents indicate that the upper chambers were used as sleeping quarters. These chambers were simply furnished with stools and straw-filled mattresses that lay on the floor. But servants spent little time in their sleeping chamber. They had too much work to do elsewhere.

The loft above the upper chambers was an important storage area. Quantities of goods are often mentioned in the historical record. While root vegetables, cider, and beer would have been stored

Nailing this escutcheon, made of copper and other metals, around the keyhole of a chest protected the piece of furniture from scratches.

In 1962 Henry Chandlee Forman unearthed a fancy, glass garment button (back and front sides shown upper left) in St. John's backyard. A buckle, believed to be a hat buckle (back and front sides shown bottom left), was also discovered in the backyard. Both items had enameled backs and a similar design. Together, they create a still-unsolved mystery: Were they part of a matched set? And if so, had both adorned a hat or another article of clothing? Just as a person sewing today does, a colonial woman (sewing was considered women's work in those days) protected her finger from the needle's point by placing a thimble (top right) on her fingertip. Rarely are seventeenth-century colonial iron needles with the eye still intact found. Perhaps Anne Lewger or one of her servants used this needle.

in the large cellar beneath St. John's parlor, harvested corn had to be stored in a dry place and as far away from hungry mice as possible. The loft above the sleeping chambers was a perfect spot. Accessed via a ladder that could be removed, Anne stored dried ears of corn there until she needed them. John might have stored court records upstairs too.

Building St. John's house took thousands of hours of work, but when it was completed, the laborers could rightly be proud. From cellar to loft, it was a comfortable home with luxuries that most houses lacked. It provided safe, warm shelter for the Lewgers and their servants. But it was more than a home. St. John's was a hub of provincial business and a working plantation with fertile land that seemed to promise wealth. Attaining wealth, however, was not easy.

GROWING GOLD

Seventeenth-century English adventurers who immigrated to Maryland hoped they would strike it rich growing American gold—tobacco. For hundreds of years, American Indians had cultivated the variety of tobacco native to the Chesapeake region and smoked its bitter leaves during religious ceremonies and on formal occasions. John Rolfe, an English planter today mostly remembered for being married to Pocahontas, brought sweet tobacco seeds from the West Indies and Venezuela to Virginia. He discovered that sweet tobacco grew well in the Chesapeake's climate, and it quickly became the region's most important commercial crop. In England, smoking became fashionable for all classes, rich or poor. American planters happily supplied the growing English demand.

The historical record is awash with documentary evidence that any Marylander—a carpenter, a tailor, a blacksmith, and even a provincial secretary—who had access to a couple of acres of land grew tobacco. As soon as the land at St. John's was ready, John Lewger told his servants to plant tobacco.

Growing tobacco demanded year-round work. Planters sowed seeds in raised seedbeds during February. In late spring or early summer, they transplanted the seedlings to knee-high hills where they remained until the leaves fully matured. During the summer, servants weeded the tobacco and pulled off the plant's lowest leaves. This forced nutrients into the plant's upper leaves making them grow larger and increasing their value at market. Autumn chores included harvesting the stalks and hanging them on scaffolds inside a tobacco house where they hung until dry, about four to six weeks. Daily, the men checked the leaves for signs of mold that would destroy the leaves. Finally, the men bundled the leaves into wooden casks called hogsheads. A hogshead filled with tobacco weighed about 400 pounds (180 kilograms). By 1640 Lewger was one of the largest tobacco planters in the colony.

Field laborers thinned the tobacco seedlings that were growing in the raised beds in late March or early April. Summer was also pest control time. Workers handpicked the leaf-eating larvae of horn- and cutworms from the tobacco leaves. Robert Serle, the Lewgers' youngest servant, may have spent many hours doing this chore.

Space left between drying tobacco leaves allowed air to circulate around them. This helped prevent mold from growing on the leaves.

Given its heavy weight, rolling a filled hogshead was not a task for the fainthearted. A full hogshead could easily crush a person's arm or leg.

Tobacco is almost always mentioned in documents concerning financial transactions in seventeenth-century Maryland—not surprising since tobacco was, essentially, the colony's money. Colonial Marylanders paid wages to hired workers and purchased goods with tobacco. The amount paid or owed depended on how much English money it took to buy a specific quantity of tobacco at the time. For example, a good carpenter expected to be paid 20 pounds (9 kgs) of tobacco per day. In 1639 an estate inventory document of storekeeper and planter Justinian Snow includes a secondhand shirt valued at 16 pounds (7 kg) of tobacco and a used pair of shoes at 12 pounds (5 kg). For 800 pounds (363 kg) of tobacco, you could have purchased the indenture of Snow's servant Christopher Morland. A cow cost up to 1,000 pounds (454 kg) of tobacco, a breeding sow about 150 pounds (68 kg), and a hen about 7 pounds (3 kg). Of course colonists didn't carry barrels of tobacco with them when they shopped.

To ensure that gold or silver had not been shaved from a coin (thus reducing its value), merchants compared the coins they received with coin weights like this one. Different coin weights were the exact weights of specific denominations of coins. The presence of this coin weight is evidence of the business trading that occurred at St. John's.

"In reality, little actual 'money' or its surrogates circulated in the economy. It was a credit economy of debits and credits—not unlike ours," Silas Hurry explained.

Men and women willed tobacco to their heirs. Borrowers and lenders kept records of pounds of tobacco owed and paid. John Lewger recorded many court cases in which colonists sued one another for unpaid tobacco debts or other pledges of tobacco.

Written records of tobacco crops and of the various financial transactions are abundant, but tobacco also left its mark in the archaeological record. Tobacco leaves go up in smoke leaving no trace, but pipes are solid evidence that offer a wealth of information.

Pipes found at St. John's came from three sources: England, the Netherlands, and those made in the Chesapeake area. Wealthy colonists imported pipes made of white clay from Europe. The pipes made with the reddish local clays are called terra-cotta pipes. Native Americans made the oldest pipes found at St. John's. Some English and African immigrants who didn't have money to spend on imported pipes also began using local clay to make their own pipes, but the vast majority of local pipes were made by Indians.

Fragile pipes often broke when smokers tapped out ashes or dropped them. Archaeologists seldom find complete pipes and find many more fragments of stems than bowls. But even the fragments of stems and bowls can help archaeologists date the stratigraphy of a colonial site such as St. John's house. "Pipes are dateable in several ways," Henry Miller explained. "The size and shape of the bowl is a key way of dating. They were small and bulbous early on, since tobacco was expensive. Bowls gradually became larger over time; by the end of the 1600s, the sides became straighter."

A pipe can also be dated if the maker stamped it with an identifying

Decorating terra-cotta pipes became fashionable in the seventeenth century. A colonial pipe maker embellished the pipe on the left with a heart. A Native American pipe maker meticulously inscribed the pipe on the right with the image of a deer.

mark. Archaeologists love finding these marks. "Maker's marks give us a *who*, *where*, and roughly *when* a pipe was made. For example 'EB' is Edward Bird, an Englishman who made pipes in Amsterdam in the Netherlands between 1635 and 1665. Llewellin Evans, who made pipes between 1665 and 1685 in Bristol England, stamped his pipes with 'LE,'" Miller added.

The third way archaeologists date pipes is the size of a pipe's borehole. A borehole is the straw-like pathway for smoke that a pipe maker creates when he or she pushes a wire through the pipe stem and into the bowl. The borehole is a uniform size except for widening slightly where the stem joins the bowl. By measuring the borehole of hundreds

Finding a pipe with a maker's mark is a rare treat. Knowing that Edward Bird and Llewellin Evans made these pipes told archaeologists when and where they were made.

of colonial pipe stems, archaeologists discovered that the boreholes of pipes made during the early seventeenth century were wider than those of pipes made at the end of the century. For reasons of style or perhaps just to get the heat of the burning tobacco farther from the smoker's mouth, pipe stems got longer and longer during the late seventeenth and eighteenth centuries. Henry Miller thinks it's possible that as pipe stems became longer, the size of the borehole needed to be smaller to prevent the stem from snapping apart. By considering the shape of the bowl, identifying marks, and the size of the borehole, archaeologists could compare the pipes found in the different strata at St. John's house and distinguish whether the pipe belonged to the early period of the homestead's occupation or the later period.

While tobacco was Maryland's cash crop, the corn crop was crucial in a different way. Every Maryland planter was required by law to grow enough corn to feed those who lived on his or her land. Historians estimate that men ate about three barrels of shelled corn per year, women ate about two and a quarter barrels of it, and children ate slightly less than one barrel. About 2 acres (0.8 hectares) of corn per worker was necessary to meet this need. John Lewger received part of his salary in barrels of corn from the crop owned by Cecil Calvert. So the workers at St. John's may not have planted as much corn as those on other plantations did. Throughout the summer, the men weeded the corn until it grew tall enough to shade out growing weeds. In the autumn, Lewger's servants harvested and stored the dried corn.

As the provincial secretary, Lewger received a salary from Cecil Calvert; Lewger also received income from his tobacco crop. Becoming a merchant offered a third opportunity for wealth. Located near water and the town, St. John's was ideally positioned as a center of trade. Lewger borrowed money against future profits and imported goods such as linen from England. Records from 1641 show he bought imported English goods from Richard Ingle, a shipmaster and trader. He also bought a sailboat called a ketch so he could "deliver his goods and collect tobacco." Unfortunately, Lewger was unable to sell what he purchased for enough money (tobacco) to pay his creditors.

To dry an animal hide, fur traders fastened it to a wooden frame. Sharply pointed iron hooks, called tenterhooks, held the hide in place so it couldn't shrink as it dried. Today, people still use the phrase "on tenterhooks" to mean they are nervously waiting to find out what has happened to someone or something.

English merchants often traded rumbler bells like this one to Native Americans. This bell, found at St. John's, still has the clapper inside it. The bell still rings when it is shaken.

Lewger also overextended himself in the fur trade. Clues historians have gleaned from the historical record suggest that a man named Mathias de Sousa assisted Lewger in his fur-trading venture. De Sousa arrived on the *Ark* in 1634 as one of the nine servants brought by the Catholic priests. His surname is Portuguese, but no one knows where he was born. Nor does anyone know where or when he began working for the Jesuits. But Jesuit records note that he had African ancestry. De Sousa was one of the first documented persons with African ancestry in Maryland.

Enslaved Africans, brought by Spanish and Portuguese traders, arrived in the New World during the sixteenth century. In 1619 the first Africans landed in the colony of Virginia. During the first half of the seventeenth century, the English did not commonly use the term *slave*. All African and European workers were called servants. Historians still debate the legal status of Virginia's first Africans. "There was a great transition in thought in English America during the seventeenth century," explained Henry Miller.

"While slavery existed in the English colonies, the status of Africans was not well defined. People of African heritage could be slaves or indentured servants. Documents in the historical record suggest that some of the first Africans who arrived in Virginia later became free and moved to the Eastern Shore of Maryland."

Records from 1642 show Leonard Calvert contracted for "fourteene negro men-slaves, & three women slaves, of betweene 16. and 26. yeare old able & sound in body & limbs." No evidence exists of their arrival. However, African workers did live on the plantations of other wealthy Marylanders. "Chesapeake society in the seventeenth century was unstable. It was a society with some slaves, but the majority of the laborers were Europeans," Miller added. At that time, it was cheaper to buy the indenture of a European servant than to buy an enslaved African.

For much of the seventeenth century, enslavement was not a hereditary state—a newborn baby was not automatically enslaved—nor was it always a lifetime condition. (Laws in the 1660s and the 1670s changed this.) Some masters set a length of time for an African person's servitude, though often the term was so long that freedom was unlikely. "As late as the 1670s, there are court cases of

Africans, who had served as indentured servants, suing their masters to gain their freedom," said Miller. "White indentured servants often had to do that as well." By the 1680s, Africans accounted for one-third of Maryland's workforce.

The historical record is silent on de Sousa's whereabouts between 1634 and 1639. Historians think he remained with the Jesuits for at least four years, the typical term of an adult's indentured servitude. The Jesuits often sailed to American Indian villages, where they preached Christianity and traded English goods for furs. Either on these voyages or elsewhere, de Sousa learned how to sail a pinnace, a small two-masted ship. In court testimony, he stated that during 1641 to 1642 he served as the skipper of a pinnace when he traded for fur with the Susquehannock Indians.

Stuffed with furs and other trade goods, skippers sailed pinnaces and shallops similar to the one shown here up and down Maryland's numerous waterways.

St. John's house and property as they appeared about 1642, during John Lewger's period of ownership

In 1642 he indentured himself for at least four months to John Lewger as payment for a debt he owed to Anne Lewger. No one knows why he was indebted to her, nor is the specific work that de Sousa did for Lewger mentioned in the historical record. Given de Sousa's skills, it seems reasonable to assume he helped Lewger in his fur-trading venture.

De Sousa was often inside St. John's house. In fact, a document proves he was in St. John's parlor on the afternoon of March 23, 1642. In his notes for the provincial assembly, which met there that afternoon, Lewger recorded de Sousa's name in the list of assemblymen who attended the meeting. At that time, the only requirement for a man to vote in the assembly was that he be a free man.

The record notes that de Sousa voted on the laws discussed that afternoon. The walls of St. John's house witnessed Mathias de Sousa's votes—the first cast by a person of African ancestry on American soil.

Unfortunately, years later a series of fires destroyed many early colonial records. De Sousa vanishes from the historical record after 1642, and the rest of his life remains a mystery.

By early 1643, Lewger, burdened with debts, quit his labors at being a merchant and fur trader. He leased his trading ketch to Thomas Cornwaleys, one of the original colonists, a member of the provincial council, and the wealthiest man in the colony, for 43 pounds (20 kg) of tobacco per day. Unfortunately, Lewger was still unable to completely recoup his losses. In April 1643, to satisfy his remaining debts, he mortgaged St. John's freehold, its house, and all its buildings to Cornwaleys for a loan of 10,000 pounds (4,353 kg) of tobacco. Cornwaleys permitted the Lewgers to continue living there. After that, John Lewger focused his undivided attention on provincial matters and the care of his tobacco fields. Anne Lewger, meanwhile, focused her attention on raising the children and managing St. John's house and its yards, chores that occupied her and the other women at St. John's day and night.

Mathias de Sousa's name is recorded in the minutes of the provincial assembly for March 1642. In this document, his name is abbreviated as "Matt das Sousa."

Keeping House

U nless a planter had a shortage of servants, only men worked in the fields. Running a household and overseeing work done in the surrounding yard was considered women's work. At St. John's, Anne supervised her servants, Martha, Ann, and Mary. Within a year of moving into St. John's house, the Lewgers had so many chickens that they could afford to give Cecil Calvert fifty or sixty of their breeding hens "at any time." Feeding the chickens and collecting eggs was a regular task for the women at St. John's.

They also cared for the Lewgers' livestock. As was the custom, the Lewgers' hogs and cattle ran loose in the countryside, where they foraged for food on their own. Owners identified their livestock by cutting a pattern of notches, each pattern unique to an owner, into the ear of each animal.

Foraging livestock destroyed food crops. Considering the long hours Anne's servants spent caring for the kitchen garden, she wanted fences that were horse-high, bull-strong, and pig-tight. St. John's fences vanished long before the walls, and nothing in the historical record mentions them. But the archaeologists found their ghostly whispers in the soil. All the fences that surrounded the yard were made by setting wooden posts—and sometimes a part of the fence—into the ground. Over time, the posts and

The chickens that roam a living history farm at St. Mary's City wander outside the house during the day and roost in their coop at night. In colonial times, feeding chickens and collecting eggs was work usually done by women and children.

fences rotted, leaving behind stained soil. Hundreds of years later, the trowels of Garry Stone's crew scraped the soil surface and uncovered the postholes that had held fence posts.

They also uncovered a long, uninterrupted line of stained soil along the outer side of some of the fences. These stains represented ditches. "The ditch and fence combination was common. The soil from the ditch was pushed up and mounded around the fence making it more rugged. The ditches we found were a very early way of dividing land, so they probably date from John Lewger's time," explained Henry Miller. "I think these rugged fences surrounded the garden and orchard area of the yard, perhaps to keep out deer which are very hard on young apple trees. When we planted the orchard at St. Mary's living history plantation museum, we lost quite a few trees because deer nibbled on the shoots and ate the young leaves."

Slowly, the archaeologists revealed patterns of stains that showed exactly where the old fences had stood. The stratigraphy of overlapping stains told them the order in which the fences were built. And the backfill in the postholes and ditches dated to the time when each fence was built. As long as the backfill hasn't been disturbed, any artifacts it contains must date to that time period or earlier. Items such as a sherd of Indian pottery, a broken bottle from Anne's kitchen, or construction debris from later home renovations all helped the archaeologists to determine when the various fences were erected.

In the seventeenth century, a pale (picket) fence (above) neatly edged a kitchen garden or a yard. Today, the evidence of two long-gone fences is a soil stain shaped like an X. The two fences did not exist at the same time. The later fence just happened to cut across the line where an earlier fence once stood.

Colonists constructed wattle fences by weaving long, thin wooden poles around upright fence posts.

The zigzag pattern of split-rail fences formed a barrier that prevented hogs and cattle from trampling crops.

FILLED DITCH →

← FILLED FENCE TRENCH

Fence posts once stood in the trench outlined by the thin line of dark soil. The wider dark line represents a ditch dug alongside the fence.

𝒢host fences were not all that the archaeologists found in the yards. They found more ghost walls. In the backyard, adjacent to the parlor, archaeologists uncovered postholes that outlined a building that had been 19 feet (6 m) long by 15 feet (5 m) wide. After analyzing and dating the artifacts found in the oldest layers of their excavations, they deduced the structure was probably built while John Lewger owned the house, possibly in the early 1640s. Based on references in the historical record, they concluded the building served double-duty as a servants' quarter and a storage house. Although certain soil stains suggested the structure might have had a wooden floor, the absence of artifacts such as window glass and plaster indicate that it lacked the frills of the main house. At one time, the building had a brick fireplace and chimney. But the stratigraphy and the artifacts found within the layers of soil and rubble established that the brick fireplace was too recent for the Lewger period and was an addition made by a later renovator.

The women at St. John's cared for cows, poultry, and the kitchen garden every day, but that was only part of their work. Preparing dried corn kernels so they could be cooked as mush or used in bread baking was women's work. Documents in the historical record indicate that by 1639, a mill existed on Mill Creek, less than a fifteen-minute walk from St. John's. Anne may have sent kernels to the mill for grinding. If not, Martha, Ann, or Mary ground them with an iron pestle inside a wooden mortar. Grinding corn was monotonous, boring, and exhausting—a chore so despised that some indentured servants added a clause to their contract that specified they would not grind corn.

Grinding corn was a much-disliked task. The boy is holding a riddle, a hoop covered with loosely woven cloth. The user sifted ground corn through the riddle. Finely ground corn sifted through. Corn that didn't sift through was tossed back into the mortar for more grinding.

To grind corn, a woman poured a small amount of kernels into the mortar; then she lifted a heavy iron pestle as high as she could and dropped it onto the kernels. She repeated this action until the kernels were crushed fine enough for cooking. It took about ten minutes to grind one cup of cornmeal. To grind enough corn for everyone who lived at St. John's, the servant raised and dropped the heavy pestle hundreds, if not thousands, of times. Women who ground corn regularly developed strong muscles in their shoulders and upper arms.

Anne Lewger directed dairy chores: milking the cows, churning butter, and making cheese. After milking the cows, one of the maids carried the buckets to the dairy. She poured the milk into a shallow ceramic milk pan, about the diameter of a medium-sized pizza pan, where it remained until the cream rose to the surface. Then she skimmed the cream from the surface and poured it into a butter churn, a slender wooden barrel, about thigh-high, covered with a wooden lid. A wooden paddle's broomstick-like handle poked through a hole in the lid's center. Dashing the paddle up and down, the maid churned the cream until it solidified into butter.

These are fragments of a milkpan found at St. John's. It is made of red clay and has a clear, shiny lead glaze. The rim of the largest fragment has been slightly pinched to form a spout for pouring milk and cream from the pan. The drawing is a cross-section view of a complete milkpan.

While butchering hogs and cattle was considered men's work, women usually prepared the meat afterward for storage by salting, hanging, and smoking it. As was customary, Anne and her servants stewed food in a kettle hung above the kitchen fire or cooked it in a skillet placed on an iron stand that stood near the embers. The residents at St. John's feasted on pork, chicken, beef, a variety of fish, wild fowl, small mammals, and deer. In England, where deer were scarce, only the nobility ate venison. In Maryland, where deer were plentiful, everyone, even the children, ate it. The historical record contains no menus of the meals served at St. John's, but plenty of bones that belonged to these animals have been found on-site.

Sometime about 1650, a colonist wounded the deer this bone belonged to. The bone healed around the bullet, proving that the deer continued to live after it had been shot.

Oyster shells are also plentiful at St. John's. While some had been used during the house construction, most of them were scraps left over from meals. Colonial documents mention that oysters found in the region were too big to eat in one mouthful. Some archaeologists wanted to know if that was really true, so they measured the size of discarded oyster shells found at several colonial Chesapeake sites. They discovered that the size of the oyster shells decreased as the population of colonists increased and the demand for oysters grew stronger. In other words, the people harvested the oysters before they could grow very large. Later in the century, when the population of colonists shifted to other regions of Maryland, oysters were less in demand and the trend reversed. The same trends hold true today for fishing of all types.

In the seventeenth century, people commonly ate with spoons and knives. The spoon (top left) is made of a metal called pewter. Forks did not become popular until the 1700s. But someone on the cutting edge of tableware fashion used this folding fork (top right) at St. John's. While a knife's blade was made of metal, the handle was often made of bone. This bone knife handle, found at St. John's, split into two pieces (above center). The knife's tang fit into the notched slot in the handle. The image directly above is a nineteenth-century bone-handled knife. It shows how a metal blade is fastened to a bone handle.

Unlike colonial women in New England, Anne and her maids did not weave cloth, nor did they dip or mold candles. Marylanders imported almost all manufactured goods, such as cloth, candles, and shoes, from England. Making these items would have diverted time and energy from supplying the needs of those who were busy growing tobacco.

Caring for the Lewger children—John Jr., Cicely, and baby Ann—was Anne's responsibility. There were few English children in the colony during its earliest years, so the Lewger children didn't have many playmates. But after the age of six, colonial children didn't have much free time for play. They had too many chores to do.

Being the master's son, John Jr. would not have worked long hours in the fields, as Robert Serle may have. But John Sr. would have expected his son to understand how to grow and cure tobacco, since it was an important part of the family's livelihood. John Sr., the most educated man in Maryland, made sure that his son could read and write. He also taught him how to survey land. Documents in the Maryland archives confirm that John Jr. did all of these things. Anne probably kept young John busy with farmyard and household chores, such as gathering firewood and carrying buckets of water. When old enough, Cicely and baby Ann would be expected to mend clothes, prepare food, and perhaps collect eggs.

As the residents of St. John's carried on their daily lives, they produced garbage. And as we do today, they disposed of items they couldn't reuse or repair. Unlike us, they couldn't put their garbage at the curb for pickup. Instead, they

A chess pawn and a die, both carved from animal bone, prove that seventeenth-century life at St. John's wasn't all work and no play.

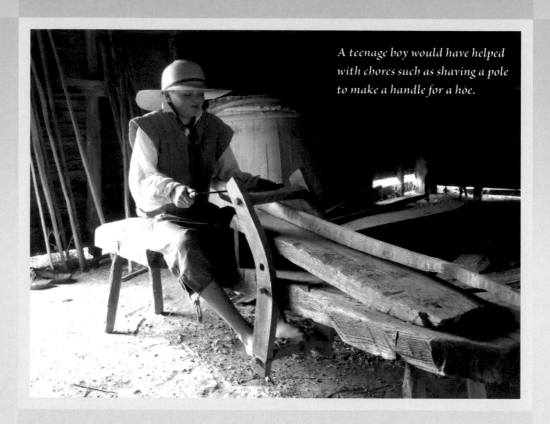

A teenage boy would have helped with chores such as shaving a pole to make a handle for a hoe.

tossed it out the closest door or carried it to a trash pit somewhere in the yard. Today's investigators didn't learn this from written documents. They found the evidence buried in St. John's front yard and backyard. Colonial trash has become an archaeological gold mine. Artifacts and other materials found in St. John's trash pits helped the scientists determine when the trash was deposited and even how the household's eating pattern had changed over time.

The bones found in a trash pit are a great indicator of diet. When archaeologists examine bones, they first determine if the bones are still articulated—connected together as they would have been during the animal's life—or if they are all mixed up. Articulated bones indicate that the entire skeleton was buried at once. Since a person pulls bones apart as she or he chews or cuts off meat, bones discarded after a meal are seldom, if ever, articulated. And a stewed or boiled carcass falls apart as it cooks. "Some of the bones we found had axe cuts, and sometimes they even had the shallow side-by-side groves where a person had carved off slices of meat. By knowing the type of animal and the specific bone, I can tell if a bone [discovered in a trash pit] was part of a ham, a sirloin steak or a rump roast. While we will never know the name of the person who ate the meal, we can know precisely what and how they were eating centuries ago," Henry Miller explained. "Bones tell many stories—types of livestock, butchery and cooking methods, even the

Colonial workers tossed their trash outside the door. Areas to the right and left of doorways are prime trash pit locations. Many broken pieces of pipes and tableware were found adjacent to the doorways of the main house and the structures in the front yard and backyard. This woman is wearing a vest and a petticoat covered by an apron. The long-sleeved shift she wears beneath extends down to her calves. Women wore their shifts as nightclothes just as men did. At all times, women wore some type of head covering.

This trash pit at St. John's held a hodgepodge of artifacts. The large pottery fragment is part of a milkpan. An iron spur is at the far left. The neck of a bottle, oyster shells, and fragments of pipe stems are to the right of the large milkpan potsherd.

nature of the environment—if we take the time to decipher and read them." St. John's trash pit treasure trove yielded some surprises. Since hogs are so frequently mentioned in the historical record, colonial historians thought pigs were the most significant source of the colonists' meat. But St. John's trash told a different story. The bones excavated from them proved that, over time, as the number of cattle at St. John's increased—as noted in the historical record—beef became over two-thirds of the meat the colonists ate. And the pit's stratigraphy further aided the archaeologists in determining that St. John's residents ate more wild game during the summer, since it was plentiful at that time of year.

Even though St. John's house was among the finest houses at St. Mary's City, in one respect it was like all other colonial houses: no toilets. Everyone either stepped outside when they had to go to the bathroom or, when it was nighttime or the weather was bad, they relieved themselves in a container, often called a chamber pot. The container's contents were later dumped. But the archaeologists were tickled to find evidence of a structure that, despite many excavations at St. Mary's City, has only been found at St. John's.

In St. John's backyard, Garry Stone's archaeologists removed soil layers of what had been a large pit. "Several layers contained significant amounts of fish and other bones. There was a spear point made of a rock called rhyolite in one of the layers. In other layers we found several ceramic pieces, pipes, bottle glass, and other items discarded as trash," explained Silas Hurry.

At the bottom of the pit, about 3 feet 8 inches (1 m) below the ground surface, a dark layer of mounded soil, unlike the overlying layers, intrigued the archaeologists. "Hoping to learn more, we carried out the first scientific study of soil chemical distributions on a seventeenth-century colonial site," Henry Miller stated. Soil scientist John Foss and

This spear point, made of rhyolite, is among the oldest artifacts at St. John's. It is between twenty-eight hundred and four thousand years old. As luck would have it, the point was probably tossed into the privy pit when someone was shoveling dirt into it. Since rhyolite is found in western Maryland, the point's presence confirms long-distance trading in ancient times.

archaeologist Robert Keeler analyzed the soil's chemistry. They discovered that the mounded layer at the bottom of the pit was very high in chemical compounds called phosphates. Phosphates are found in organic waste matter. The soil at the bottom of the pit had ten times more phosphates in it than the trash-filled layers above it. Foss told the archaeologists that human feces and urine caused the soil's unusually high phosphate level. Although its walls were long gone, there was no doubt: St. John's house had a privy!

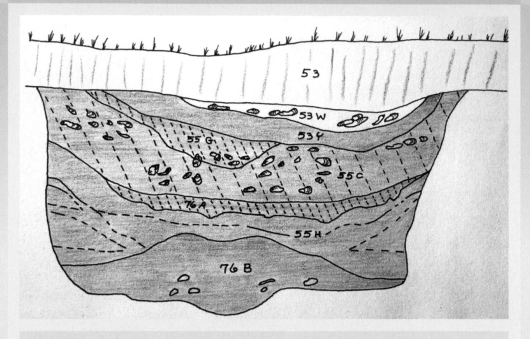

An archaeologist's cross-section diagram (top) illustrates the privy's stratigraphy shown in the photograph (below).

Key for diagram:
53 = plowed soil layer
53W = secondary trash deposit 1660s
53Y = clay fill layer to level ground
55G = fireplace ash deposit with some trash
55C = garbage layer of oyster shell, animal bone, charcoal, pottery, etc., ca. 1650

76A = ash, charcoal, and some trash
55H = trash and clay soil washed in from the sides of the pit
76B = dark organic rich soil layer from privy use, with a few shells

Also called an outhouse or "the necessary," the privy was a small wooden structure. Situated above a pit, the occupant sat inside, perched over a hole cut into a wooden shelf. Then the occupant took care of business, so to speak, letting waste matter fall into the pit. In later years, when the privy was no longer used, the pit remained. People threw trash into it until the pit was full.

Maintaining St. John's property, livestock, crops, house, and even the privy was essential for the survival of the Lewger family and their servants. But St. John's house was equally important for the colony's survival. It was an essential provincial building. Men governed Maryland within its walls; they resolved many legal issues, murder among them, in St. John's parlor.

DECISIONS

ST. JOHN'S PARLOR was the seat of a busy young family, but it soon became more than that. On February 25, 1639, it became a seat of power when Governor Leonard Calvert officially moved government operations, such as assembly meetings and sessions of the provincial court, from his house inside the fort to St. John's roomy parlor. Settled in chairs and on benches, the colony's politicians lit their pipes and got to work.

Assembly meetings often got rowdy. So, their first order of business in the Lewgers' home was setting ground rules. When in session, the assembly would meet twice daily: the morning session began at 8 o'clock; the afternoon session began at 2 o'clock—Sundays and holy days excepted. Representatives who were absent for roll call were fined 20 pounds (9 kg) of tobacco. When discussing provincial business, the assemblymen had to take turns speaking, one at a time. Leonard Calvert cautioned them, saying "No man shall . . . refute another with any nipping or uncivill terms." The walls of St. John's house listened as the assemblymen discussed crime and punishment, American Indians, standardizing weights and measures of tobacco, planting corn, servants, livestock, the militia, and oaths of allegiance to King Charles and Cecil Calvert, the lord proprietor.

The lord of any Maryland manor could convene a court on his property to settle minor disputes that occurred on his land. But larger disputes over property or crimes such as murder and theft required St. John's walls.

In February 1643, planter John Elkin was tried for entering onto land owned by the Yaocomaco Indians, where with "malice aforethought," he shot

There's no doubt that St. John's parlor was smoke-filled during assembly meetings. Everyone—even young teens—smoked. Curved grooves formed in the teeth of smokers who constantly held a pipe stem clamped between them. (The pipe stem wore away the tooth surface.) Some grooves were so large that the smoker could push a pipe stem into the resulting hole without opening his or her jaw.

and killed the Indians' leader. As provincial attorney, John Lewger submitted into evidence Elkin's signed statement in which he confessed to killing the American Indian man. The jury decided Elkin should be tried for murder.

Elkin pled not guilty and the jury acquitted him. They justified their verdict stating that the American Indian man was a pagan (not Christian) and that no trial in Virginia had set a precedent for an American Indian who had been killed under this circumstance.

Lewger believed that legally this verdict was incorrect. He told the jury that the Yaocomaco were people "in the peace of the king & his Lordship [Cecil Calvert]." Furthermore, he told them not to base their verdict on what courts in Virginia had or, in this case, had not done. Instead, the jurors should follow the "Law of England." He instructed the jury to reconsider its verdict.

The jury's second verdict was "guilty of murther in his owne defence." Lewger advised them that this was a contradiction in terms: murder is a premeditated killing by definition. And self-defense would only apply if the American Indian had been trying to kill Elkin, which was not what had happened.

Again, Lewger asked them to reconsider. Their third verdict found "that [Elkin] killed the Indian in his owne defence." This verdict completely disregarded Elkin's confession. Disturbed, Leonard Calvert, who was the judge, declared a mistrial and ruled "that the verdict be not entered as a verdict, but that another Jury be charged to enquire & try by the same evidence." The jurors for the new trial found Elkin guilty of manslaughter. Lewger's and Calvert's refusals to accept a verdict of not guilty at least tried to place American Indians and Englishmen on equal footing in the eyes of the law.

One year later, St. John's walls overheard the murder trial of John Dandy, St. Mary's blacksmith and gunsmith. Nails that he forged held the walls and floor of St. John's parlor—the courtroom—together. Unfortunately, Dandy's temper was as hot as the fire in his smithy.

In February 1644, John Lewger issued a warrant arresting John Dandy for the murder of an American Indian boy named Edward. Under court orders, the coroner and a panel of freemen investigated the death and reported their findings. After examining the body, they testified that Edward died three days after receiving a gunshot wound in his abdomen and that John Dandy was the man who shot him. In court, Dandy pled not guilty. After hearing the evidence, the jury convicted him of murder. Dandy was sentenced to death by hanging.

Ironically, guns saved Dandy's life. The colonists needed his skills as a gunsmith. Respected people signed a petition requesting clemency. When Leonard Calvert, who had been absent when the trial occurred, granted the petitioners' request upon his return, he based his decision on the "many good services performed by [Dandy]" and various matters he had undertaken "for the good, & safety of this Province." Three years later, Dandy's death sentence was commuted to seven years of servitude. A man who could make nails and guns was simply too valuable to kill.

The historical record preserves a great many explicit, grim facts about life in the past, but it can also offer tantalizing hints and reminders that the men and women of the past had personalities. Words that John Lewger wrote while sitting at his desk in St. John's parlor do offer historians insight into not only his personality but also that of Cecil Calvert.

Historians know that Cecil Calvert, despite never having visited Maryland, kept himself well informed of his colony's political, religious, and economic issues. They learned this by reading letters that Calvert and others wrote. They gleaned additional information about him from official transcripts of various provincial meetings. These documents revealed Calvert as a principled and pragmatic man. But they also learned that Calvert was a curious man, interested in Maryland's flora and fauna. Sometimes this created headaches for John Lewger. England needed timber; Maryland had plenty of trees. However, Calvert's multiple requests for cedar, which he hoped might be a profitable commodity, stymied Lewger. "For the Cedar desired, I know none here worth sending, as I told your Lordship by my last [letter]," Lewger wrote to Cecil in January 1638.

Calvert's requests for specimens of Maryland's animals similarly failed. A mountain lion, captured on his behalf by his brother Leonard, had died. And his request for a redbird seemed to test Lewger's patience. Swamped with a lot of provincial business and little time, Lewger wrote, "For the birds, I have no cage to putt them in when they be taken, nor none about me dextrous in the taking of them, nor feeding of them, & I have my selfe so litle leisure to look after such things, that I can promise litle concerning them."

Cecil Calvert even asked Lewger to find and send him the two American Indian arrows that the king required Calvert to pay annually for the ownership of Maryland. There, Lewger drew the line. "I scarce see an Indian or an arrow in halfe a yeare neither when I doe see them have I language enoughe to aske an arrow of them." From Lewger's letters, historians learned that while he conscientiously carried out his professional duties, he was not inclined to spend his time satisfying Calvert's curiosity.

Rarely does the archaeological record confirm a specific notation in the historical record. It's like finding the proverbial needle in a haystack. Luckily, it happened at St. John's.

Wolves that preyed on the colonists' livestock were a major problem. So much so that the provincial government paid a bounty of 100 pounds (45 kg) of tobacco per wolf head. A number of animals owned by Cecil Calvert, sheep among them, lived on John Lewger's property. In 1643 Lewger wrote that wolves killed one ewe, two lambs, and a ram from Cecil's flock housed at St. John's.

In 1973, in St. John's backyard, archaeologists unearthed the skeleton of a pregnant ewe. She was buried in a shallow grave about 25 feet (8 m) from the kitchen door. The bones of two unborn lambs lay in her abdominal area.

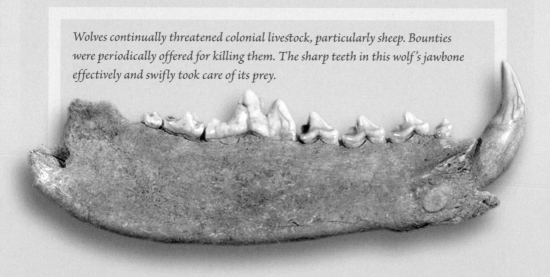

Wolves continually threatened colonial livestock, particularly sheep. Bounties were periodically offered for killing them. The sharp teeth in this wolf's jawbone effectively and swifly took care of its prey.

Using a dental pick, Henry Miller patiently reveals the skeleton found in one of the sheep burials (left) unearthed at St. John's. Another sheep burial (below) contained the remains of a ewe and two unborn lambs. The fine, thin bones in the central portion of theses remains belong to the unborn lambs.

Henry Miller is sure this is one of the sheep Lewger noted in his report. Forensic evidence supports him. A large portion of the ewe's skeleton was present and still articulated. Had the sheep been cooked and eaten, its bones would have been disarticulated, like the bones found in St. John's trash pits. But the ewe's hindquarters (with the exception of one small lower leg bone) and the skull of one lamb skull were missing. While the blade of a farmer's plow could have dragged some of the bones away, most of the bones were buried deeper than a plow's blades. None of the bones have cut marks from a butcher's knife, nor were there any clear tooth marks on the bones. But one of the bones in the ewe's lower back was damaged. "I believe the most likely explanation is carnivore activity. A wolf probably killed her and then carried off her hindquarters," said Miller.

He added further evidence, "Other than the bones, there were few artifacts in the soil that filled in the grave. Only a fragment of a square bottle and a crumb of the red brick used to build John Lewger's chimney." It is logical to assume that if the ewe had been buried during the later part of the seventeenth century, when English artifacts were plentiful, some of them would have ended up in the soil used to backfill the grave. "Their absence suggests the ewe was buried during the early days of occupation at St. John's, between 1638 and 1660," Miller concluded. Perhaps, someday, yet undiscovered evidence from either the historical record or the archaeological record will provide proof that confirms the scientists' theory.

In the seventeenth century, the survival of St. John's house and its people depended on many colonial decisions. In the twentieth century, archaeologists found themselves faced with decisions that would determine whether their ghost of a house had a future at all.

As St. John's archaeological dig expanded, the site needed more permanent protection from the weather, other environmental conditions, and even careless visitors than plywood sheets or tarps could provide. Discussions began for building a museum. But St. John's fragile chimney bricks and a cellar prone to flooding couldn't wait for the time it would take to plan, finance, and build a permanent museum. St. John's needed a stopgap solution.

In 1973 the pounding of hammers at St. John's echoed the construction

The A-frame stands sentinel over St. John's foundation while the archaeological crew excavates and screens new material in the yard.

days of 1638 as modern-day carpenters began work. "Garry Stone erected an A-frame around the foundation. The frame was covered with plastic sheeting that could be rolled up each day for ventilation," recalled Henry Miller. This worked fine for a couple of years. But wear and tear shredded the plastic sheeting. So the carpenters replaced the sheeting with fiberglass panels and built a wooden walkway, with viewing ports, inside. They also added a door with a lock. "The panels protected our excavations while allowing visitors to see the original remains. We unlocked the door while we worked and for special tour groups. Schoolchildren visited a lot during the late 1970s and 1980s," Miller explained. "The A-frame was only meant to last for a few years, until funding for the permanent exhibit was available." But raising the necessary funds, plus the bureaucratic delays that occurred when the St. Mary's people had to wait for legislative approval—something John Lewger would have understood—took years. Decades passed as St. John's ghost walls waited for new museum walls.

As frustrating as the wait was for archaeologists and historians, it paled in comparison with misfortunes that tore apart seventeenth-century Maryland and its residents, especially the Lewger family.

By 1642, political differences between King Charles and Parliament had exploded into civil war. Like most aristocrats and Catholics, Cecil Calvert supported King Charles and his Royalist troops. Still, Calvert had to remain sufficiently in the good graces of Parliament, which had the power to revoke his charter for Maryland. Meanwhile, the tension between Marylanders who supported Parliament and those who supported the king skyrocketed. Maintaining Calvert's policy of liberty of conscience became increasingly difficult.

In 1644 trader Richard Ingle, who supported Parliament, arrived in Maryland from England. He made statements about King Charles I that angered Leonard Calvert and other influential Maryland Catholics. Their accusations led to Ingle being tried for treason. Ingle's anger in the trial's aftermath ultimately led

When praying, Roman Catholics use the beads of a rosary like this one to help them count a specific number of devotional prayers. This rosary was found in the backfill of St. John's cobblestone foundation trench, so it dates to the original construction. It was likely put there to bless the house—perhaps it even belonged to the Lewger family.

A colonial corkscrew? No. Sometimes a musket failed to fire. A musketeer extracted the jammed lead ball from the musket's barrel with a musket worm like this one. Attached to a rod, he screwed the sharp spiral into the lead shot and then pulled it out.

to a year-long rebellion that derailed the Calverts' rule of the colony.

In 1645 Ingle and his followers—mostly Protestant colonists—looted and even burned the homes of Catholic colonists. One night, they stormed St. John's house, seized Lewger, and took him away clad only in his nightshirt. One of the men "in compassion of his [Lewger's] nakedness gave him a pair of shoes and stockings" taken from their stash of plundered goods. Ingle imprisoned Lewger on board Ingle's ship and took him bound in chains to England, where he was detained for nearly a year.

When Lewger returned to St. John's, in the spring of 1646, the freehold still suffered from the rebellion's effects. Looters had taken goods from the house, ransacked the tobacco houses, and stolen or driven off most of the family's livestock.

This is part of a seventeenth-century dagger. It is called a pommel, a piece located at the base of the dagger's grip. Made of iron, the pommel is decorated with an image of a human head. If you look closely at the lobe on the right, you can see eyes, the nose, and the mouth. The iron was coated with silver plating (the gray-colored material) for a fancy appearance.

Lewger's losses far outweighed his remaining assets. Losing St. John's freehold was a very real possibility.

In the rebellion's wake, a Protestant provisional government controlled the colony's day-to-day operations. Many fearful Catholics had fled the province. Many Protestant planters who had lost money when tobacco prices plummeted in the early 1640s had moved elsewhere, too. Fewer than two hundred colonists remained in Maryland. (Six hundred to seven hundred colonists lived in Maryland prior to Ingle's rebellion.) Lewger resumed his provincial duties as best he could, while hoping that Leonard Calvert, who had fled to Virginia during the rebellion, would soon return.

The Lewger family's reunion was short-lived. Anne Lewger died in 1646. The historical record is silent about the cause of death, but historians think it's possible that she died during childbirth, a not uncommon fate for colonial women. Where Anne is buried is also unknown, but it's reasonable to assume that she was buried in the cemetery outside the Catholic chapel in St. Mary's City. When Anne died, her son, John, was still a teenager. Cicely and Ann were both younger than ten.

By December 1646, Leonard Calvert and his soldiers had regained control of the government. But John Lewger no longer had the heart for living in Maryland. In 1647 Lewger resigned his provincial duties. Leaving his son in charge of St. John's, Lewger and his daughters sailed to England, where he became a Catholic priest employed as Cecil Calvert's private chaplain.

Colonial records note that after Lewger's departure, Leonard Calvert strove to put Maryland's government back on an even keel. However, he died on June 9, 1647, after a short illness. While not specifying his cause of death, documents do state that on his deathbed, he appointed Thomas Greene governor. Then, surrounded by official witnesses, he did something unexpected: he appointed a woman named Margaret Brent, the sister of influential Catholic colonist Giles Brent, to be his executrix and said, "Take all, & pay all."

In seventeenth-century England, a married woman's wealth belonged to her husband. But because she was unmarried, wealthy Margaret Brent controlled not only her money but also her land (she and her sister both owned manors), crops, and livestock. Leonard chose her deliberately. One reason was because Margaret was intelligent and had a keen sense of business. During provincial court sessions in St. John's parlor, she represented herself, the affairs of her ward—a Piscataway Indian girl named Mary Kittamaquund—and even those of her brother Giles. Leonard knew Margaret could ably administer his estate. The second reason he chose her was because English society demanded that men treat a well-bred lady, such as Margaret, with respect. Leonard trusted that Margaret would diplomatically safeguard Maryland until Cecil could send instructions.

Leonard was scarcely buried before the soldiers who had aided him in regaining the colony began hounding the provincial court for outstanding wages, a total of 13,000 pounds (5,987 kg) of tobacco and twenty-eight barrels of corn. Had Leonard been alive, he would have paid the soldiers with Cecil's American assets. The provincial court did not have the authority to do that, yet waiting for Cecil's authorization would take months. Acting on its own, the court appointed Margaret to act as Cecil's attorney. Fearing Cecil's disapproval, Margaret hesitated to disburse his assets. But if she didn't, the soldiers might mutiny and the whole colony would be lost. She stalled the soldiers while she considered her decision.

At the same time, Margaret made all the financial decisions regarding Leonard's personal estate. She attended provincial court sessions. She sat through assembly meetings. As she sat in St. John's parlor, Margaret realized that she was doing the same duties that the assemblymen did—even more, when she considered that the court had appointed her to act as Cecil's attorney. In fact, the only thing she didn't do that the men who attended the exact same meetings did was vote.

"The important thing to understand is that in Maryland, the Assembly really was democratic until the 1650s, in that any free man could participate. It was not like in Virginia, where only rich guys became the representatives. If Margaret had been a man, she would have had a vote as a landowner for sure. Women unfortunately could not vote," explained Henry Miller.

On January 21, 1648, the walls of St. John's house witnessed a bold request, one that still exists in the historical record: Margaret told the assembly that she wanted to vote. Furthermore, she didn't request one vote; she asked for two: one in her own right as a free landowner, the other for acting as Cecil's attorney. Thomas Greene, the governor, denied her request. Before she left St. John's parlor, Margaret registered a protest against all Calvert-related decisions made by the assembly unless she was given the votes she had requested.

The soldiers' demands for payment grew more strident; mutiny seemed inevitable. Margaret sold some of Cecil's cattle and paid the soldiers. Her decision forestalled mutiny and saved the colony.

Despite having denied her request to vote, the assembly wrote Cecil Calvert a letter that expressed support for Margaret's action, noting that the soldiers respected her with a civility and respect that they would not have offered to any man after Leonard's death. They informed Cecil that he owed Margaret Brent "favour and thanks."

Margaret's request to vote was highly unusual in seventeenth-century English politics. During the eighteenth and nineteenth centuries, select wealthy and influential women—but only in a few states and under specific circumstances—were allowed to vote in elections in colonial America and later the United States. It wasn't until 1920, when the Nineteenth Amendment to the United States Constitution was passed, that all women who are US citizens were guaranteed the right to vote.

After his father left Maryland, John Lewger Jr. lived in St. John's house and charged the government a fee to hold meetings in the parlor. For three years, he struggled to turn around the family's monumental rebellion losses. Despite a rise in tobacco prices, his efforts were unsuccessful. In 1650 he conceded defeat and sold St. John's house, all its outbuildings, and the property to Henry Fox for 5,000 pounds (3,268 kg) of tobacco. Half the tobacco he received went toward settling his family's debts. Lewger left St. Mary's and later established a plantation about 45 miles (72 km) northwest of St. Mary's City. He married, had three children, raised crops, and sometimes worked as a surveyor.

Henry Fox, the new owner of St. John's house, was a former servant who had worked his way up the economic ladder to become a planter and merchant. During Fox's ownership of St. John's, the assembly and provincial court no longer met in the parlor, but the house was occasionally used for other governmental purposes. For a fee, Fox provided room and board for people who were waiting for their trials to be heard in the provincial court. And in 1654, the governor designated St. John's house "for the prison of the County of St. Maries."

Henry Fox's business ventures proved unsuccessful. In 1654 he sold St. John's house and property to Simon Overzee, a rich merchant. During Overzee's ownership, the walls of St. John's house witnessed growth, anguish, death, and theft.

a merchant MOVES IN

Although only in his mid-twenties, Simon Overzee was well-established in America when he bought St. John's. Born in England about 1628, he was the son of Dutch parents. Overzee followed in his father's footsteps, becoming a merchant and trader. When he arrived in Virginia, in 1649, he already co-owned a Dutch trading ship. A shrewd businessman, Overzee involved himself in various ventures. He bought land, operated a store, and profited from both. He also married Sarah Thoroughgood, the daughter of a prominent Virginia planter. In 1651, intent on increasing his wealth, the historical record notes that Overzee moved Sarah and their baby to Maryland, where he bought more land, eventually owning three plantations. With his numerous business pursuits in full swing, Overzee was often away from St. John's house. Sarah and the child remained behind.

Like most new homeowners, the Overzees made changes at St. John's house. The historical record provided a few details about their modifications. During their first year in the house, a letter written by carpenter John Crabtree stated that Overzee promised him and his helper "five & fifty pownd Sterl[ing] in England & five thousand pownds [2,268 kg] of Tob[acco] & cask here in Maryland" for work done at St. John's. At a rate of 20 pounds (9 kg) of tobacco per day, this more than paid the wages of two carpenters for four months' work. By comparing the amount of money that Overzee owed Crabtree with comparable sums paid for work done at other plantations, Garry Stone and Henry Miller speculate that big projects, such as building tobacco houses (for drying harvested plants) or re-siding the house were under way at St. John's. In the same letter, Crabtree wrote that he planned to come and lay floors in the house. But he died in 1655, shortly after writing the letter. Whether his helper completed the flooring is unknown. However, Stone's twentieth-century crew of archaeologists shed a lot of light on what some of the Overzee's renovations included, as well as their taste in material goods.

Excavating a dig is all about removing younger materials to expose older ones that lay buried beneath. While Stone's crew was removing the soil that had covered Anne Lewger's cobblestone dairy floor, they discovered that the artifacts found in that soil dated from the mid to late 1650s. This is when the Overzees owned the house. From this, they knew that the Overzees were responsible for filling in the small dairy. The historical record doesn't contain a list of the goods that the Overzees owned. However, analyzing broken sherds of pottery provided evidence of their taste in material goods. The archaeologists

Archaeologists found many sherds of blue and white pottery (below right) that date to the period when Simon Overzee owned St. John's. Made in the Netherlands during the seventeenth century, these plates were often decorated with colorful lines, dots, and swirls. Some even featured images of animals and people. Although the colorful, complete plate (below left) was not found at St. John's, it was manufactured with a process similar to the plates owned by the Overzees.

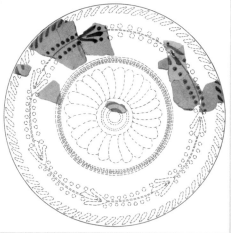

found a lot of Dutch pottery that dated to the 1640s and the 1650s. During England's civil war, which occurred during those years, fewer trade ships sailed from England to America. Dutch traders—men like Simon Overzee—quickly took advantage of the void and brought Dutch goods to America.

Overzee cleared more land behind the house than the Lewgers had cleared. In the far northwest corner of the backyard, he added a structure that stumped the archaeologists when they first found it in the 1970s. The pattern of postholes suggested an open-front shed, perhaps for keeping sheep. Unsatisfied, the archaeologists continued asking what else it could be. When additional excavations were conducted from 2001 to 2005—in anticipation of building the long-hoped-for museum, which was still in the planning stage— the archaeologists widely excavated that area. One reason they did so was to try to answer their question about the mystery building and its use. A second and perhaps more time-sensitive reason was to uncover, identify, and record as much archaeological evidence from any areas that might be impacted by the museum's construction.

"Inside newly revealed postholes, we discovered remnants of the black locust timbers used to construct the building. Black locust is a high-quality timber. Only locust and red cedar have been preserved in certain postholes at St. Mary's City. Other woods just do not last centuries in this soil. Using this quality of timber is rare and shows the structure was built of good materials," Henry Miller explained. "More importantly, it turned out that our 1970s work had only uncovered three-fourths of the structure. By missing one entire wall, it had looked like a shed with an open side." New postholes revealed the complete structure: a four-sided building with narrow, 3-foot-wide (1 m) aisles. The discovery overturned the team's earlier theory concerning the building's use.

"The aisled building still remains a bit of a mystery. If it had been larger, we might have considered it a hay barn. Its construction mirrors Dutch farm buildings. But the interior configuration is strange because such narrow aisles are not useful for livestock of any size. However, poultry is small, so it's possible it was a henhouse," Miller added. Additionally, the building's location, between the house and the orchard, was close enough to the main house to make egg-gathering convenient. "Until more analysis is done, the best we can say is that it was a farm building."

Although the farm building mystery wasn't solved, another 1970s mystery was. In July 2004, crew member Wesley Willoughby was at St. John's screening buckets of plow zone soil removed from one of the squares sheltered inside the A-frame structure. "I picked up from the screen what I thought was just a plain oyster shell—of which we were finding a lot since they were used in plaster wall construction. It was the general size, shape and color of oyster shell so I initially didn't think anything of it. Out of habit, I rubbed off some of the larger chunks of dirt adhering to it before placing it in the appropriate artifact bag. Then I realized it had some unusual features and textures. As I cleaned more dirt off, it became apparent that it was a face molded out of white pipe clay, a very rare and unusual find. We brought the specimen back to the lab at the end of the work day and showed it to Silas Hurry," said Willoughby.

"When I saw the angelic face [and the curls], it reminded me of another artifact that had been found at St. John's during the 1970s excavation. We took the new fragment and opened the drawers which held the material dug up in the 1970s," recalled Hurry.

"Silas pulled the original piece out to compare with my new discovery. Lo and behold, they matched and formed the complete head!" Willoughby said. The complete head answered the archaeologists' earlier question of what the object really was. It was a putto, a work of art that depicts a chubby, male infant. And at last, they knew exactly what the missing face looked like.

If ever a discovery made the St. John's archaeologists want to shout, "Eureka!" it was Wes Willoughby's completely unexpected find.

Even as one old mystery was unsolved, the 2001 to 2005 excavations uncovered another: a tiny building incorporated into a fence. "This strange, square building, about 10 feet by 10 feet (3 m by 3 m), stood not far from the farm building. We found daub associated with it, so it likely had wattle and daub walls. But the building's architecture is not typical English or Dutch. I think it may be of American Indian or African origin. At times, Indians and Africans worked at St. John's," Henry Miller stated. Might these workers have contributed building practices from their cultures? For now, this question remains unanswered.

As the crew excavated the cellar area (at the parlor end of the house), they discovered an exterior entrance to the cellar and evidence of a stairway that descended into it. Stratigraphy and datable artifacts enabled them to assign these renovations to the Overzees.

In St. John's front yard, excavations revealed postholes that outlined a large storage building, about 30 feet (9 m) by 20 feet (6 m). "Documents indicate that Overzee was planning on expanding his commercial activities in the late 1650s, so he probably built a solid, but unheated, storage building," Miller said. Overzee needed a dry storage space for hogsheads of tobacco and other goods. The storage building in the front yard provided safe shelter and was close to his boat landing on Mill Pond for easy transfer to larger trading ships. Some of the artifacts associated with the building dated from the mid to late 1650s, when Overzee owned the house.

The historical record contains additional glimmers about St. John's house and outbuildings while the Overzees lived there. Three testimonies given in provincial court trials, mention the kitchen, a dairy, and a backyard quarters. One suggested that Sarah Overzee's kitchen was inside St. John's house in 1658.

A second testimony noted that a maid came into the house from the diary. A dairy outside the house would have made Anne Lewger's dairy obsolete, so workers backfilled it. Testimony in a different trial, in 1656, stated there was "a negro woman in the quartering howse" in the backyard. These testimonies provided details of St. John's house and its physical appearance. But they also told two chilling stories: one inside the walls of St. John's, the other in the front yard.

Renovations were not the only changes wrought at St. John's during the mid-1650s. Indentured servants had always lived at St. John's. The Lewgers, Henry Fox, and the Overzees all contracted with indentured servants. Only Simon Overzee increased his workforce by purchasing American Indian and African laborers. De Sousa had willingly indentured himself for a limited time to Anne Lewger. It is not clear whether the American Indian and Africans that Overzee bought were servants or enslaved people. But there is no question that he sometimes dealt dishonorably with them.

In 1651 a man named John Babtist worked at Overzee's plantation at Portoback Creek, about 50 miles (80 km) northwest of St. John's house. According to Henry Miller, "Court proceedings recorded that Babtist was 'a Moor from Barbary,' which is an area of northern Africa. Culturally speaking, he was different from the sub-Saharan peoples who were most often brought as captives to America." Babtist was especially interesting to Miller because he was the first person of North African origin in Maryland. Miller said, "He is likely the first person of the Muslim faith in Maryland. On different occasions, Babtist certainly spent time at St. John's, further adding to the remarkable cultural diversity found among its seventeenth-century inhabitants."

Two years later, Babtist petitioned the court for his freedom, stating that Overzee brought him to Maryland, but not for lifetime servitude. Babtist stated that he'd already served at least five years, a traditional term of indenture. In 1655 Babtist was back in court again, still in servitude. The court ruled that Overzee owed Babtist a year's supply of corn and a suit of clothes, which were his freedom dues. Then the court fined Overzee 1,800 pounds (816 kg) of tobacco for seven months of false service. The court's ruling implied that Overzee had forced Babtist to work seven months longer than he should have. "We can assume that Babtist did not part on good terms with Overzee,"

St. John's house and property as it appeared during Simon Overzee's ownership in the mid to late 1650s.

Miller said. And the fact that in 1661 Babtist yet again petitioned the court for the corn, clothes, and tobacco proves that Overzee had not honored the court's order. Babtist's problems with Overzee paled when compared with those of another man, who Overzee certainly considered as an enslaved person for life.

Antonio did not willingly come to Maryland. Enslaved in Africa and brought to America in bondage, he arrived in Maryland in March 1656. While not 100 percent certain, a paper trail of shipping documents and court records plus well-known trade ties between certain colonial settlers suggest likely links in a chain of events that led to Antonio's enslavement and transport to America. Shipping records show Dutch traders Jan Sweerts and Dirck Pietersen Wittepaart co-owned the sailing ship *Wittepaart*. In November 1654 the Dutch India Company approved their request to buy enslaved Africans in what is now the Republic of the Congo and transport them to New Amsterdam (New York City). There, they would be sold to promote the "population growth and the improvement of the aforesaid place."

In early 1655, traders forcibly loaded 455 enslaved African men and women onto the ship. Of these, 64 died before *Wittepaart* docked in New Amsterdam, in September. Virginian Edmund Scarborough, a wealthy planter and merchant, also owned thousands of acres of land in Maryland. He purchased at least 41 of the Africans. In early 1656, he transported them directly to Maryland.

At that time, fewer than two hundred Africans lived in Maryland. News of Scarborough's large purchase would have spread quickly. Documents show Scarborough often traded with Dutch merchants and Overzee brought Antonio to Portoback Creek in March 1656, shortly after Scarborough brought the Africans to Maryland. It is reasonable, then, to conclude that Scarborough and Overzee knew each other and that Overzee purchased at least one African person from Scarborough—namely Antonio. Two years later, in court, Job Chandler, Overzee's brother-in-law and co-owner of Portoback, testified that in 1656, he "could not perceive any speech or language hee [Antonio] had." This suggests that Antonio had recently arrived in America and spoke no English.

Enslavement for Africans and others was not legally defined in Maryland until September 1664, but it seems clear that Overzee regarded Antonio as his property and not an indentured servant. When Overzee brought him to Portoback Creek, Antonio actively resisted his enslavement and refused to work after Overzee left. Job Chandler told the plantation's overseer that if Antonio couldn't be persuaded to work by "fayre meanes" to "give him blowes."

The document below is an extract from the register of resolutions kept by the directors of the West India Company, Chamber at Amsterdam, translated from Dutch, No. 26. 9:

November 1654. Messrs. Jan de Sweerts and Dirck Pietersz Wittepaart appeared before the assembly, requesting leave to go from here to the coast of Africa with their ship Wittepaart for slaves, and to trade the same in New Netherland upon payment of the ordinary tunnage or impost affixed thereto. Upon questioning, lengthy discussion took place; and finally, as it was understood that the same would tend to promotion of population growth and the improvement of the aforesaid place, the same was allowed them, provided that the Company shall have the option, upon the arrival of the aforesaid ship, which must return here, to collect the proper imposts on goods, which it is carrying, or the ordinary tonnage, according to the regulation enacted on the coast of Africa. Whereby the aforesaid Messrs. Jan de Sweerts and Dirck Pietersz Wittepaert are satisfied. Agrees with the aforesaid register, in the absence of the advocate, C. van Seventer.

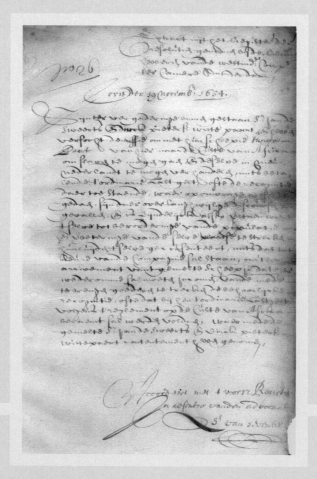

Twice Antonio ran away from Portoback, only to be recaptured. The second time, Chandler noticed that one of Antonio's fingers was badly infected. Claiming Antonio was "a dangerous Rogue" who might harm him or his family, Chandler ordered the overseer to take Antonio straight to St. John's, where his finger could be either medically treated or cut off so that he didn't lose his arm or even his life to gangrene. Rather than improve, Antonio's life worsened at St. John's. Testimony shows that in September 1656, Sarah Overzee had ordered Antonio placed in chains for "some misdemeanors."

When eventually Simon Overzee released Antonio and ordered him back to work, Antonio lay on the ground in St. John's front yard and refused to stand. That was when Overzee cut sticks from a nearby pear tree and whipped him and then threatened to stab servant William Hewes if he tried to help Antonio. That was when Overzee ordered servant Hannah Littleworth to heat a small shovel. Overzee melted lard in the shovel and then poured the hot lard on Antonio's bare back. Afterward, Overzee ordered an enslaved American Indian to tie Antonio— arms stretched high above his head—to the ladder that leaned against the walls of St. John's house. And then Overzee let Antonio hang until he suffocated.

Word of Antonio's death spread, and echoes of that news remain in the historical record. Two years later, in December 1658, Simon Overzee was tried for "correcting his negro servant." In February 1659, Hannah Littleworth and William Hewes testified in court. After deliberation, the jury returned their verdict: *ignoramus.* This legal term, Latin for "We are ignorant" or "We ignore it," meant that the jury found the accusation against Overzee groundless. Overzee was acquitted.

Obviously, Overzee's actions led to Antonio's death, so why was he acquitted? In the 1600s, a master could legally beat a servant or an enslaved person with a stick, as long as the stick's diameter was smaller than the thickest end of a man's finger. Littleworth testified that the pear sticks were "to the bignes of a mans finger att the biggest end." And as long as no blisters appeared, a master could pour hot lard on a servant. Littleworth testified that the lard was hot, "but not soe hot as to blister any one." Hanging a person by the wrists was also legal, provided the person's feet touched the ground. The court asked Littleworth and Hewes if Antonio's feet were on the ground, "Yea or Noe?" Littleworth said yea; Hewes said that as best he could remember, they "stood upon the grownd." Legally, the jury had no choice but to acquit Overzee.

In 1658, as autumn approached, Simon and Sarah Overzee looked forward to the birth of another child. When Sarah began labor, she sent for Mary Clocker, the local midwife, who lived a couple of miles away. Simon was away on business, but Job Chandler was staying upstairs in one of the sleeping chambers. Although Clocker was an experienced midwife, complications occurred. On October 9, Sarah died in her bed in St. John's parlor after giving birth to the baby. Daniel Clocker, Mary's husband, built Sarah's coffin. Mary Clocker and Mary Williams, an Overzee servant whose husband

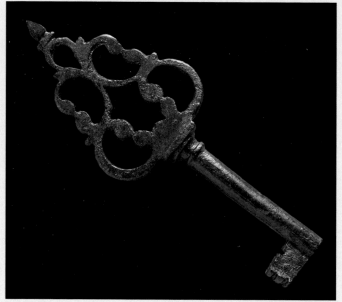

This small decorative key was used to lock a chest or another piece of furniture. Colonial homemakers kept valuable material such as spices, sugar, and lace locked up.

This iron lock once graced a trunk used to store goods at St. John's. How or why it was removed from the trunk is a mystery.

managed St. John's plantation, prepared Sarah's body for burial. Later court documents suggest that the baby died while still a toddler.

Both women disliked Simon Overzee. On the Sunday morning that Sarah's body was carried away for burial, the two Marys planned to steal a number of Simon Overzee's possessions.

Mary Clocker said, "Hang him [Overzee], If we doe not doe it wee shall never have any thing [as payment] for our paynes [in taking care of Sarah and the baby]."

Mary Williams pointed out "that these things could not be used here but they would be knowne."

Mary Clocker replied, "Rather then ever hee shall have them, I will burne them . . . [or] bury them in a Case in the Grownd."

Pretending she needed spices for a pudding, Mary Williams asked Job Chandler for the keys to the Overzee's large, two-drawer trunk kept in the parlor. (Spices were kept under lock and key because they were very expensive and difficult to get.) While the others attended Sarah's burial, the two Marys unlocked the trunk and stole linens, silver buttons, fabric, clothes, handkerchiefs, soap, gloves, sugar, and silver and gold lace. They smuggled the goods out under their skirts. Mary Clocker brought the baby to her house, since she was its wet nurse. Several days later, they stole more items from a cabinet.

Enraged by the theft, Overzee demanded the Marys' arrest. Overzee claimed they had stolen fifty pounds sterling worth of goods—only five pounds less than Crabtree's entire fee for renovating St. John's. Before the arrests, most of the goods had been recovered and returned to Overzee. At their trial, the two Marys were found guilty and sentenced "to hang by the neck till they bee Dead." Shortly afterward, for political reasons, the governor pardoned them and all other prisoners in the province who had been sentenced to death.

The two trials that centered on crimes committed at St. John's house during the time it was owned by Simon Overzee provide several examples of how information from the historical record can complement and even expand information revealed by archaeological excavation. From testimony given during Antonio's trial, historians and archaeologists learned that Overzee had at least three servants, Hannah Littleworth and William Hewes among them. He also had at least two enslaved people, an American

Indian man and an African woman. In her testimony, Littleworth said that an African woman had remained inside the backyard quarters while Overzee beat Antonio.

Testimonies given during the two Marys' trial provided several of the few existing descriptions of the interior of St. John's house. Archaeologists had wondered if evidence they found of a wattle and daub chimney that had been added to the quarters in the backyard meant that the Overzees had moved the kitchen out of the house, a practice that became common for large colonial homes. But actions that took place during the theft implied that the kitchen was still in the main house. Testimony proved without question that

The Lewgers and the Overzees housed servants in the building in the backyard and also used it for storage. Later owners replaced the wattle and daub chimney with a brick one, and the building was used as a kitchen.

Sarah and Simon Overzee used the parlor as their bedroom, as had John and Anne Lewger. Likewise, Job Chandler's presence in an upper sleeping chamber confirmed how the second story was used. Court records also verify that the Overzees built a new dairy separate from the house. During the trial, Mary Williams stated that she had gone out to the dairy to churn butter. The timeline that the scientists were establishing with their excavations dovetailed with descriptions contained in period documents.

Historians often revisit documents like court transcripts not only to reread the main ideas of the text but also to search for any incidental information the writers might reveal. In this way, testimony at a murder trial may hold the key to something as unrelated as reconstructing the floor plan of a house, for example.

That Simon Overzee was harsh, disagreeable, and unfair to some of his servants is indisputable. But with those he considered his equal or better, it seems he could be sociable when he wanted to be. He occupied a prominent position in the colony. He had many business associates, including a partnership with Augustine Herrman, a well-known trader who first arrived in Maryland as an ambassador for New York's Dutch government. On at least one occasion, Overzee translated from Dutch to English an important letter and other documents sent by Peter Stuyvesant, the director-general of the New Netherland colony (now New York), to Maryland officials. Overzee socialized with people who were politically powerful. Overzee invited Herrman to stay at St. John's house, and he dined with Philip Calvert, Cecil Calvert's youngest brother, who was then Maryland's provincial secretary and judge.

As did most colonial widowers, Overzee remarried after Sarah's death. His marriage, however, was short-lived: Simon Overzee died suddenly in February 1660. Later court testimony stated that at the time Overzee died, he had no heirs. So the child who had accompanied Simon and Sarah to Maryland and the baby born in St. John's parlor must have died before Simon. Elizabeth, Simon's widow, kept the property for only a year. She remarried and moved to Virginia, probably leaving the care of St. John's in the hands of tenants. But the house soon had a buyer. Elizabeth and her husband sold the house and the adjacent 800 acres (32 hectares) to a man who was on his way from England.

THE GOVERNOR'S HOME

Excitement grew in St. Mary's City as the ship carrying the colony's new governor dropped anchor in the river. St. John's house anticipated the arrival of its new owner, the man who would restore its political and social status. Not only would St. John's house be the governmental seat and governor's residence, it would be the home of Maryland's future lord proprietor—in a sense, St. John's house would be a colonial palace.

When Cecil Calvert's twenty-four-year-old son Charles and his wife, Mary, arrived in Maryland, in September 1661, St. John's was a twenty-two-year-

Charles Calvert, who became the third Lord Baltimore, was Cecil Calvert's son and heir. He lived in Maryland for twenty-three years and lived full-time in St. John's house until 1666.

Although quite worn, the Calvert family coat of arms is depicted on the face of this small lead object found at St. John's (above left). It is the only artifact found at St. Mary's City with the Calvert coat of arms. This book clasp (above right) fastened onto a strap attached to the covers of a book. The clasp held the covers tightly closed, protecting the book's pages inside. During his time at St. John's, John Lewger had been the most educated man in Maryland. There is no doubt that both he and Charles Calvert owned books. Perhaps the clasp is from one of their books.

old complex of buildings that had been influenced by English, Dutch, and possibly African and Native American construction practices, along with some Chesapeake innovations.

With a house to be organized, a garden to be weeded, and chicken and cows to be tended, there was no shortage of work for Mary and her servants. Equally busy, Charles assumed his new job as provincial governor—the title once held by his uncle Leonard—on November 26, 1661. The next day, after the parlor had been tidied from the previous night's supper and sleep, jurors filed into the room, Charles called the provincial court in session, and St. John's was once again the center of governmental activity.

Cecil Calvert continued to manage Maryland long-distance. He sent letters to Charles that contained instructions for governmental policies, land grants, tobacco, and trade issues. But he also sent gifts to his family. Cecil shipped books to his son, the receipt of which Charles acknowledged with appreciation. A doting grandfather, he sent his four-year-old grandson, Cecilius, presents of a "Capp feather Sword & Belt" in 1671. And as it had with John Lewger, Cecil's curiosity about Maryland's wildlife continued. Just months after Charles arrived at St. John's, Cecil asked for four elk calves—two male, two female—probably with an eye toward establishing a herd in England for profit. Like John Lewger, Charles tried to obtain them but finally admitted, "I have used all my endeavours possible but can procure none as yet." In fairness, elks probably did not rank high on Charles's list of priorities. Charles's time was fully occupied. When governmental duties didn't claim his attention, managing St. John's house and property did.

Again, St. John's walls echoed with life as the Calverts settled in and renovated. And as before, two kinds of digging pieced together what some of those changes were.

In 1974, while Garry Stone's archaeology crew removed soil at St. John's, historian Lois Green Carr and her team dug through three-hundred-year-old documents in the Maryland State Archives. One day, she telephoned Stone with stupendous news.

"It was more exciting than receiving a Christmas present," Stone recalled. "Russell Menard, one of her team members, had found a document written in 1678 between Charles Calvert and an innkeeper named Henry Exon, who wanted to lease St. John's for seven years. The lease included a list of repairs that Exon was required to make in the house and on the property, proving those changes occurred after 1678." Stone continued: "As a result, we had to rethink some of our old hypotheses. For example, based on the available archaeological evidence, I previously concluded that Charles Calvert had greatly modified the house in 1662. Those renovations, however, were on the 1678 list of reparations. I had to correct my old hypothesis. Equally thrilling, the list included the names of structures we had not yet found—in essence, they were presents still waiting to be opened."

During excavations in 1974, Stone's crew uncovered soil stains in the backyard that supplied the evidence of an early fence. Abruptly, near the kitchen, the clear fence line disappeared. Instead, the archaeologists found a pattern of postholes that outlined a small addition to the back of the house—a room, about 11 feet (3 m) by 10 feet (3 m). Was it a shed? Further excavation exposed bricks, plaster, and stains that suggested the presence of a wood floor, all of which seemed lavish for a simple shed. The stratigraphy and the datable

NURSERY WALLS

MAIN HOUSE FOUNDATION

Anticipating the birth of a child, Charles and Mary Calvert added a room onto their home. Postholes supplied physical evidence of the room; the historical record supplied information about the room's intended use.

artifacts they found strongly supported the room having been added during the 1660s, so it was neither a Lewger nor an Overzee renovation.

The 1678 list of reparations came to the rescue. One of the items on the list was to repair the "Room called the Nursery." The room needed its foundation shored with bricks, its plaster walls patched, and its roof replaced. Mention of a separate foundation and roof imply that the room was an addition. Together, the physical evidence and information from the historical record fixed the room to the Calvert period and disclosed its purpose: Charles and Mary Calvert were expecting a baby.

But tears followed months of joyful anticipation. Mary died while giving birth—the third woman to die in childbirth in St. John's parlor. That her death occurred in 1663 seems to be confirmed in a letter Charles wrote to his father in April 1664. In it, he stated that his cousin Anne Calvert (Leonard's daughter) had arrived from England and "has the care of my houshold affaires." Anne would not have been placed in charge of the house if Mary had been alive.

Being in charge of St. John's household while Charles Calvert was governor was a demanding task because he frequently entertained important visitors. In the same letter, Charles lamented to his father that he had thirty people to feed and house at St. John's, "which does putt me to some care & trouble." Even though Mary had recently died, Charles had to uphold his governmental duties and his responsibilities as the owner of St. John's.

St. John's house as it appeared during Charles Calvert's ownership, circa 1666

In St. John's trash pits, archaeologists unearthed pieces of fine Chinese porcelain and Venetian glass vessels that date to the years from about 1650 to 1675. "Simon Overzee was wealthy, so some of the items could have been owned by him. But Charles Calvert was the most elite resident who lived at St. John's," said Henry Miller. "It's known that he entertained members of the Governor's Council at St. John's and he would have done so in style." Considering his status, it seems certain that Calvert owned elegant, expensive tableware.

The Calverts and their guests ate well, but the identification of the small addition as a nursery caused the archaeologists to consider yet another

 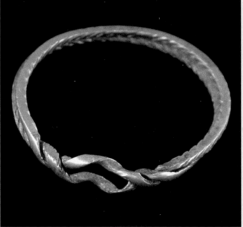

This gracefully styled fragment of glass (left) once adorned the base of an elegant drinking glass used by one of St. John's residents. Only the wealthiest colonists could afford glass of this type. A goldsmith made this delicate ring (right) by twisting and hammering two strands of gold wire together.

renovation, this time a kitchen update. "Given the Calverts' need for space to entertain guests and their social status, they may have decided that a separate kitchen would better serve their needs," Miller explained. "Plus, the fact that the nursery is off the large room at the west end of the house—the room the Lewgers and Overzees had used as a kitchen—suggests it was not being used as the main kitchen when the Calverts lived at St. John's. If the Calverts were using the room as a hall, or second sitting room, the baby's nursery was close at hand."

If Miller's theory is true, where did the servants prepare meals? "We found a large daub pit just outside the door of the servants' quarter in the backyard. It was filled with materials that dated from about 1660 to 1665. Charles's workers did something to the chimney, even if it was only to repair an existing wattle and daub chimney. My guess is that Charles moved the main kitchen to the quarter in the backyard." The 1678 list of repairs included repairing "the room called the Kitchen and the Store and [the] chamber over them." As with the nursery, the combined archaeological and documentary evidence support Miller's conclusion.

Charles Calvert also renovated other buildings near the house. "Unlike Simon Overzee, Charles was not a merchant, so he did not need a large storage facility in his front yard. Our excavations uncovered the remains of a brick fireplace and chimney that had been added to the storage building. Charles needed to care for a lot of people and he needed space to accommodate them. It makes sense to conclude that he would have readapted the storage structure as a heated living quarter," said Miller. Postholes suggest the quarters had two rooms, but it did not have a stone foundation or glazed windows. The front quarters may still hold secrets about its construction and use. But in keeping with St. Mary's City standard practice, the archaeologists left part of the front quarters unexcavated for future investigators who might bring to bear new tools and techniques.

On the land outside the yards, established apple, pear, and peach orchards produced fruit, enough that Charles could send his father dried peaches. Following Cecil's instructions, Charles attempted to diversify the crops at St. John's and other Calvert property in Maryland by growing English grains. By September 1663, Charles informed his father that he'd sowed "15 or 16 bushells of wheate and 10 or 12 bushells of Oats, 7 bushells of pease, and 8 or 9 bushells of Barley." Despite this yield, Charles's foray into growing English grains never succeeded as a large scale production because they couldn't compete with tobacco as a cash crop.

Periodically, the archaeologists at St. Mary's City reexamine old evidence with techniques and tools used by other scientists. In 2013 they washed some of the soil they had saved from excavations completed at St. John's in 2001 to 2005. By stirring the soil inside a bucket filled with water, lightweight sediments formerly trapped inside the soil were able to float free. Using an embroidery hoop covered with panty hose, the archaeologists scooped up the very fine particles of floating sediment and sent them to soil scientist Justine McKnight for analysis. McKnight specializes in the identification of floral remains. Among corn, nutshell, and fruit seed remains, she also found small grains that she thinks may be wheat or oats. Might some of them have been descendants of crops that Charles planted? The scientists are still analyzing and interpreting McKnight's discoveries, waiting to see if they offer new evidence about crops and planting practices, as well as the colonial diet at St. John's.

Hired help did the hard labor of St. John's makeovers.
But Charles carried out the governmental work. Upholding existing relationships between colonists and Native Americans and negotiating new ones were among his responsibilities. Charles tried to maintain good terms with nearby Native Americans. Several times, the English allied with the Yaocomaco, Piscataway, and other local American Indian groups to fight the Susquehannock. That said, decades of ongoing grievances existed between the English and their American Indian allies.

Fire-cracked rock, pottery, and projectile points provide archaeological proof that Native Americans were present on the land that became St. John's freehold. Historical documents provide proof that tribal leaders were actually inside St. John's house. Two assembly meetings between colonists and several American Indian groups occurred in the parlor at St. John's house in 1666. In April about twenty-two Indian men, representing twelve local groups met to discuss "Articles of Peace and Amity." During those sessions, St. John's walls heard Mattagund and other Indian leaders request they be notified whenever an Indian was arrested. Specifically, they wanted to know if it was for murder. The Indian leaders asked that all murderers—whether an Indian killed an Englishman or vice versa—be arrested and judged. In other words, equal treatment in the eyes of the law. When attacked by "Foreigne Indians," those who they considered enemies, they asked that they be given guns and ammunition, so they could defend their own people *and* the colonists. During those times, they asked that their wives and children be allowed to stay with the colonists for their protection. They requested the colonists to respect Indian hunting and fishing rights. Finally, Mattagund addressed a recurring grievance that affected all the local Indians. He asked that the English prevent their roaming livestock from trampling Indian corn and eating it. He concisely summed his peoples' frustration, "You come too near Us to live & drive Us from place to place. We can fly no farther let us know where to live & how to be secured for the future from the Hogs & Cattle." After debate and deliberation, the American Indians and the provincial assembly approved the treaty.

In St. John's parlor, in June 1666, Charles Calvert and three assemblyman met with Wastahunda Hariguera and Gosweinquerackqua, two Susquehannock "warre Captaines," to negotiate a peace treaty. The

Susquehannocks' relationship with the colonists and local Indians seesawed between war and peace. But the Susquehannocks' desire for assistance and protection against their enemy, the Seneca, prompted their request for the treaty. The two war captains reminded the assemblymen that many Susquehannock men had been killed while protecting English plantations from attacks by enemies along Maryland's northern frontier. Under the treaty's terms, the Susquehannock

Wastahunda Hariguera (sign of the terrapin) and Gosweinquerackqua (sign of the fox) represented the Susquehannock Indians when they signed the Peace Treaty of 1666.

agreed to surrender the king of the Potomac Indians and his two sons, who were being held hostage. They also agreed to pay for any English-owned hogs or cattle killed by Susquehannock hunters. In return, the assemblymen promised that all former crimes committed by the Susquehannock would be forgotten and "buryed in Oblivion," with the exception of the "Murder of any English not yet discovered."

"The treaty signed in St. John's house is one of the first formal treaties signed with the Indians in the English colonies," Henry Miller stated. "It was good for all sides, although by then, the Susquehannock population was not as large as it had been, so they weren't as big a threat as they had been earlier." While the treaty was a good-faith effort, expanding colonial settlements led to increased pressure and tensions between colonists and most of the region's American Indians. By 1675 colonists were once again at "warr against the Susquehanough Indians."

Professionally, 1666 was a hopeful year for Charles Calvert; it was also a significant year for him personally. And that led to major changes at St. John's.

In 1666 Charles Calvert married Jane Sewell, a
wealthy widow with children. Suddenly, Charles found himself the stepfather
of a boy and four girls. Within a year, he and his family moved from St. John's
to property Jane owned, about 10 miles (16 km) from St. Mary's City. Charles
appointed a caretaker for the St. John's property and leased the house to a sequence
of innkeepers. Despite being an inn, documents in the Maryland State Archives
prove that the house continued to be used for assembly and court meetings.

   During the early months of 1675, Charles Calvert temporarily moved
himself and his family back to St. John's "for the more Speedy dispatch of the
publique affayres, and to Keepe a nearer corespondence with the Members of
the [assembly]."

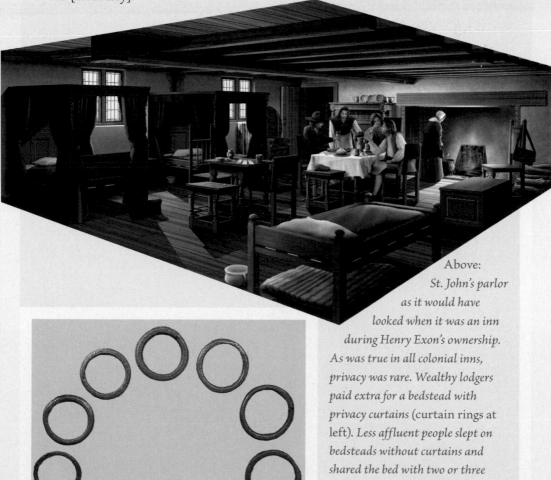

*Above:
St. John's parlor
as it would have
looked when it was an inn
during Henry Exon's ownership.
As was true in all colonial inns,
privacy was rare. Wealthy lodgers
paid extra for a bedstead with
privacy curtains (curtain rings at
left). Less affluent people slept on
bedsteads without curtains and
shared the bed with two or three
other people, usually strangers.*

Henry Exon stored special oils or a strong liquor such as brandy in a glass flask like this (top right). When complete, the flask was about 6 or 7 inches (15 or 18 cm) tall. The archaeologists were pleased to find the intact base of a small decorated bowl that was most likely used for drinking punch (top left). As excavations continued, they unearthed more fragments of the bowl, which conservators pieced together with the base (middle). Since all the missing pieces were not recovered, conservators restored it with modern materials and paint. Two of these bowls, each about 4 inches (10 cm) in diameter and 2 inches (5 cm) tall, were found at St. John's. They date to the innkeeper period and are believed to have been made in the Netherlands or Portugal.

Also in 1675, Cecil Calvert died; Charles became Maryland's lord proprietor. He sailed to England to take care of family and provincial business. When he returned to Maryland, his family permanently left St. John's house.

By the time Charles leased the house and property to innkeeper Henry Exon, in 1678, several changes at St. John's had already occurred. Its pastures and stable contained horses that belonged to lodgers. The Overzee's puzzling farm building was gone, as was the strange small building incorporated in the backyard fence. The privy was gone too. And Exon's list of repairs assured that the walls of St. John's house would undergo renovations on a scale they hadn't experienced since John Lewger's carpenters first raised them.

Garry Stone's crew knew from the list of repairs given to Henry Exon, that forty years of hard use had left St. John's house in a shabby state. Repairing the nursery that Stone's crew had excavated was only one item. Repairing the kitchen and henhouse in the backyard, fixing up the quarters in the front yard, shoring the foundation of St. John's house, pruning the fruit trees in the orchards, restoring and fencing the kitchen garden, building an oven outside (there was no indoor oven), and replacing a fence around the orchard and pasture were also on Exon's list of scheduled repairs. But two additional items—repairing the old chimney and pulling down and rebuilding the staircase—were especially helpful for visualizing more of St. John's house's interior ghost walls. Those two repairs gave Stone's archaeology crew some specific answers to questions that had arisen during their excavations.

Soon after excavations began in the 1970s, Stone's crew realized there was something odd about the big brick chimney in St. John's house: the evidence proved there had been not one but two separate chimneys in the central section of the house. Both were shaped like the letter *I*. One chimney stood in the middle of the house, between St. John's front and back walls. The other one almost touched the back wall. The archaeologists quickly determined that the chimneys had not existed simultaneously. The brickwork of the chimney closer to the back wall of the house cut through the brickwork of the chimney in the middle. Stratigraphy revealed that the chimney closer to the back wall had to be younger than the chimney in the center.

To install a new chimney near the back wall, Exon's carpenters ripped out the Lewger's chimney, the parlor closet, and the steep staircase that ascended from the kitchen. Placing the new chimney close to the back wall created a large, empty space near the front door. "This space became the entry. Carpenters built a wide, winding stairway to the upper floor rooms. With the new stairway, bedsteads, tables, and larger chests could have more easily been placed in the upstairs chambers," explained Henry Miller.

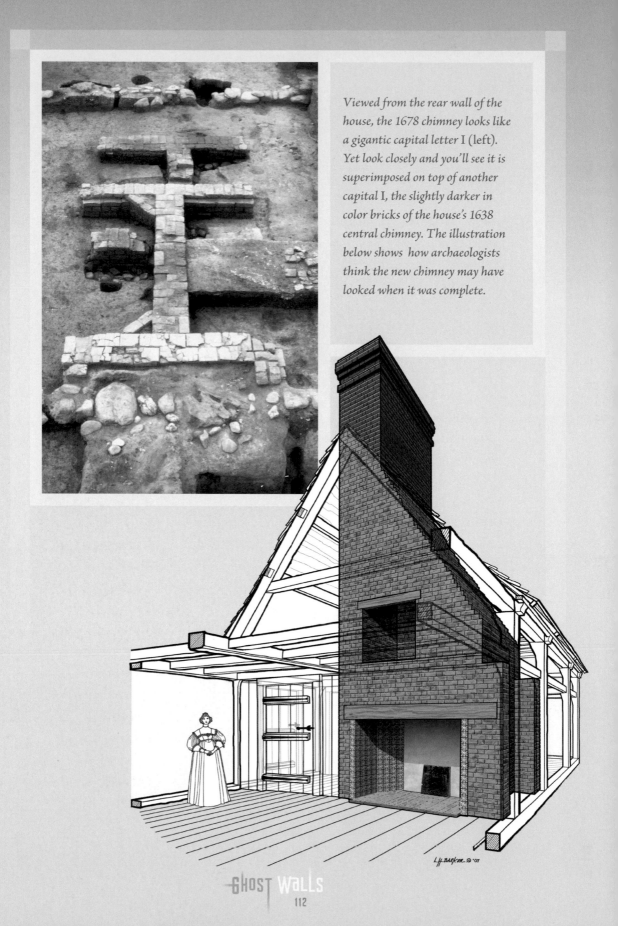

Viewed from the rear wall of the house, the 1678 chimney looks like a gigantic capital letter I (left). Yet look closely and you'll see it is superimposed on top of another capital I, the slightly darker in color bricks of the house's 1638 central chimney. The illustration below shows how archaeologists think the new chimney may have looked when it was complete.

St. John's cellar was a real stratigraphic puzzle.
During the Lewgers' ownership, the clay walls may have been lined with wood. Later, perhaps during Simon Overzee's time, the walls were lined with sandstone blocks. A section of one wall had crumbled and been repaired; another was prone to leaks. Someone paved the floor with bricks—probably Exon around 1680, since the bricks were similar to those in the new chimney.

Excavation also revealed that Exon or an earlier resident had cut a newer entrance into the cellar at the front of the house. Initially, this entrance had stone steps, but a soil ramp edged with cedar rails soon replaced them. Innkeepers rolled barrels of cider and beer—two popular beverages—down the ramp and into the cellar for storage. But archaeologists unearthed artifacts that had been thrown onto the ramp that indicate it was seldom used by about 1700.

Traces of the two cedar rails that flanked the cellar ramp still remain. It was far easier to roll barrels of cider and beer down a ramp than to carry them down a staircase.

The spaces between the bricks of St. John's cellar floor were perfect catchalls for grains of pollen.

Archaeologists at St. Mary's City always leave portions of a site unexcavated for future scientists and their technology. As a result, in 1994, twenty years after the first excavation, archaeologists could sample and analyze the soil from intact locations within the house with investigative methods not used in the 1970s. This time, they were searching for pollen, the microscopic powdery grains found inside flowers. Palynologist Gerald Kelso had told them that pollen grains might provide insight into the time of year various parts of the house were built and how the owners had used the cellar. First, the archaeologists sampled the material between the bricks of the cellar floor. Kelso found a lot of tree pollen in the material between the bricks, as well as pollen from European weeds. Miller thinks workers tracked these pollen grains into the cellar or it blew in after they installed the brick floor. The grains further suggest that trees shaded St. John's house and that foreign weeds were well established around the yard.

Next, they removed some of the bricks and collected samples from the soil that lay directly on top of the fired clay floor. The soil directly on top of the fired clay floor contained a lot of grass pollen. Miller knew that English homemakers customarily stored vegetables by packing them in straw, or the dried stalks of wheat, after the grains have been removed. Since the colonists didn't grow much wheat, it seems that Lewger's servants substituted dried grass. Samples from beneath the fired clay floor and from beneath one of the cobblestones of the main foundation of the house contained mostly tree pollen

St. John's house as it appeared around 1680, during the time Henry Exon operated the house as an inn.

and a smattering of pollen from weeds native to America. No pollen from European weeds was found in these samples, suggesting that when Lewger chose the site, it was a forested area, with limited undergrowth and no foreign plant species were yet present.

Lastly, the archaeologists sampled the soil between the cellar walls' sandstone blocks. Kelso found pollen there too. Plants pollinate at different times of the year. Oak trees, for example, produce pollen in April, while ragweed-type plants produce pollen closer to autumn. The pollen found between the sandstone blocks suggests that these walls were built over a period of six months. Microscopic evidence had provided the archaeologists with information about the site's seventeenth-century environment and a timeline for various construction projects at St. John's house.

Despite his best efforts, Charles Calvert couldn't eliminate the continuing tension between Protestants and Catholics. Upholding his father's policy of liberty of conscience was increasingly difficult. Endeavoring to retain control of the colony, Charles asserted his rights as lord proprietor. Initially, any freeman in Maryland could serve as an assemblyman, and as such, vote. Charles restricted assembly membership (and therefore, who could cast a vote) to men who owned a certain amount of land and had a certain level of wealth. Dissatisfaction increased until Protestant Josias Fendall, a man who had formerly served as one of the colony's governors, led a rebellion to overthrow Charles's rule. Charles quickly squelched Fendall's attempt and arrested him for treason. Fendall's trial would be among the last major court cases heard in St. John's house and is a historical record treasure. "Fendall's trial, held in 1681, in St. John's parlor, was the only formal trial for treason ever conducted in Maryland," Henry Miller explained. "And because Charles—the lord proprietor—wanted to make absolutely sure that a detailed record was made in case of questions or challenges from his enemies or Royal authorities, he ordered that the testimony be recorded verbatim. This is important because it is the only real evidence we have of how a major trial was conducted in the early Chesapeake." The court found Fendall guilty of treason against Lord Baltimore. He was fined and banished from the colony.

But more political changes were in the wind. William Penn's new colony of Pennsylvania was challenging Maryland's boundary lines to the north and the east. In 1684 Charles Calvert moved his family to England so he could meet with Parliament and the king and better protect his colonial territory. Charles never returned to Maryland.

As late as 1693, St. John's house still served as the probate office for wills and as a storage facility for provincial records. Two years later, when Annapolis, in northern Maryland, was established as the new capital city in 1695, St. John's house had disappeared from the historical record. Maryland's population was now nearly thirty thousand.

Neglected by tenants who had no financial stake in maintaining its upkeep, the house slowly fell apart. By 1715 people began scavenging it for construction materials to be used elsewhere; the chimney bricks were hauled away and used to build a house nearby. To prepare the site for agriculture, men filled the cellar with rubble. By 1720 St. John's house had become a ghost. But it wouldn't remain that way.

New Walls

In 2006, after three hundred years of invisibility and thirty years of planning, St. John's ghost walls were ready to swap specter for spectacular. With financing and construction permits in place, it was finally time to replace the fiberglass A-frame foundation with an innovative museum that would permanently protect the site and educate visitors about the many people who had lived there.

From the start, everyone agreed St. John's cobblestone foundation and its archaeology would be the centerpiece of the museum. "One of our goals was to incorporate the overall history of the house, and not just one owner's tenancy," Henry Miller explained.

The museum's planning committee wanted the building to convey a sense of the seventeenth century. Designing a structure that would do this as well as provide the best protection for the exposed archaeological features was a challenge. The committee quickly rejected a design with a modern appearance. "We wanted the outside of the museum to give a sense of the actual house, as it would have been seen by visitors in the 1680s. However, the museum would completely surround St. John's foundation and the backyard kitchen, so it would have to be a larger building than the original house," Miller said. "We decided the museum would have wood walls, but not clapboard, and a tile roof similar to the one Henry Exon installed. A fake brick chimney would protrude from the roof's ridgeline and we would complete the impression of a period house with simulated seventeenth-century windows," Miller continued.

The historians and archaeologists at St. Mary's City firmly believe that preserving St. John's archaeological features for future study is their duty. For this reason, stabilizing St. John's foundation and eliminating several destructive forces that were harming the archaeolgical features was crucial and had to be done before the museum's construction could start. Not doing so could have led to the site's ruin. "There was only natural ventilation in the A-frame. Since there was no climate control at all, the site's chimneys were still exposed to the temperature fluctuations during freezing and thawing weather cycles. Some of the more fragile bricks had cracked as they repeatedly contracted and expanded in response to the changes in temperature," explained Miller. Conservators treated the bricks with a protective chemical substance to prevent further deterioration.

Insects were creating problems too. Entomologist Theodore Suman discovered that termites were eating the wood and that ants, termites, and ground-dwelling species of cicadas and cicada killer wasps were tunneling around the foundation. He recommended chemical treatments to control them.

Water had eroded the clay mortar in the cellar floor and weakened the mortar joints in the stone walls. Also, the lower sections of the cellar walls had been so damp that algae were growing on them. "One of our biggest concerns and challenges for the construction period was preventing additional water damage to the site," explained Ruth Mitchell, the archaeology field director at St. John's. Geologist Gerald Johnson ascertained that the roots of a large tree at the north end of the cellar were channeling surface water—rain and melting snow and ice—into the cellar. During periods of heavy rainfall, water up to a foot (0.3 m) deep had, at times, flooded the cellar. On Johnson's recommendation, arborists cut down the tree. Workers installed gutters to channel any additional water away.

Ana Espinoza, an architectural preservation specialist, removed all the algae from the cellar walls and analyzed the damaged clay mortar between the stone blocks. She compared the clay mortar with samples of clay collected from different places around St. John's property. She found a match to the walls' mortar and used it to repair the weakened joints.

Removing algae from the cellar walls was a task given to Ana Espinoza (top). She also treated the mortar joints and refilled spaces with new clay mortar (inset).

The A-frame had to be dismantled before the museum's construction could begin.

Finally, it was time to build the museum. "The other archaeologists and I spent much of December 2005 working with the Maryland Conservation Corp preparing the site for construction. We laid out matting to protect exposed tree roots, spread a layer of blue chip stone in certain areas, and removed the old A-frame structure," said Ruth Mitchell. "Peter Rivers and Ernie Stone, members of St. Mary's maintenance staff who are skilled in covering sensitive archaeological zones, installed a large protective membrane over the foundation of the main house and the fragile bricks of the backyard kitchen. When the museum's construction crew arrived in 2006, all of St. John's archaeological features were completely covered and protected. And the contractors weren't allowed to use heavy equipment within certain areas." Mitchell watched each step of the museum's exterior construction to make sure the new work stayed within the areas that had been archaeologically cleared.

With the museum's exterior walls and roof in place, finalizing the museum's interior required careful co-ordination between the archaeologists who were uncovering colonial construction and the carpenters who were putting the finishing touches on new walls and floors. "There were careful

During the museum's construction, the foundation of the main house and the chimney of the backyard kitchen were completely covered to protect them from damage.

PARTIALLY REBUILT
FRONT WALL

TREE Ca. 1918—CUT 2005

1638 CHIMNEY BaSE

FRONT WALL FOUNDATION

1638 GROUND SURFACE

STONE CELLAR WALL

RECONSTRUCTED WEST WALL

UNEXCAVATED SOIL

1678 CHIMNEY BaSE

1972 GROUND SURFACE

UNEXCAVATED SOIL

ReaL WALL FOUNDATION

The remains of St. John's include the ruins of the original house and the two unexcavated blocks of soil, which are preserved for future study. The partially reconstructed south and west walls of the house have been added.

negotiations between the two crews. The construction workers needed to be careful of the newly exposed ruins, while I had to be careful of the new (and expensive!) glass, flooring, and wall treatments," Mitchell said.

With the museum complete and the cobblestone foundation preserved, it was time to assemble information for the featured exhibits. Even as construction had been under way, historians had collected story strands about St. John's from the historical record—Antonio's tragic tale, Native American treaties, court cases, Margaret Brent's request to vote, and sheep-stealing wolves. Scientists had chosen the story strands of archaeological objects from more than a million discoveries—including projectile points, Dutch pottery, a key, and the burial of a ewe and her young. With documents and artifacts selected, St. John's historians and archaeologists could at last weave the two story strands together and create a dynamic, imaginative exhibit. Working together, they would bring St. John's house back to life.

St. John's House, the star of the exhibit, is the biggest seventeenth-century artifact on the site. Enabling twenty-first century people to envision the house as a whole took considerable thought and imagination. "Full reconstruction of the home's walls would have hidden the original remains we wanted to showcase," explained Henry Miller. So, directly over the very fragile original foundation, using seventeenth-century building methods, carpenters reconstructed the south wall's frame and the complete west wall. Standing beside the foundation, a visitor sees how the walls linked with the cobblestone foundation, how the beams fastened together to create the upper story and loft, and how plaster was applied. Looking at the knobbly cobbles that formed Anne Lewger's dairy floor, a visitor can imagine how it felt under her feet.

St. John's is a place of history; discovery; and most of all, connections. "There is remarkable power in the actual place and its artifacts that virtual reality is incapable of offering," Miller asserts. The museum, which officially opened on September 14, 2008, contains four exhibit cases filled with artifacts that offer a glimpse into the lives of the Lewger, Overzee, Calvert, and Exon households at St. John's. The traces they left behind—a small handle from a cup, a button, teeth marks on a tobacco pipe stem, or a tiny straight pin slightly bent by a woman's hand—are proof of their presence. In other cases, pottery sherds and projectile points remind us of Native American homemakers and hunters. A fragment of an iron shackle remembers enslaved people forced to make new lives in a strange land.

The entire privy pit was reconstructed as an exhibit in the museum. Each drawer represents a stratigraphic level of the pit and contains all the artifacts found within that level. Visitors can see for themselves the kinds of materials that, over time, filled the pit.

Each item suggests something about the person who used it. In a very real sense, seventeenth-century ghosts—of people and of a place—spring back to life.

St. John's is a place that stretches your imagination. "It is the place I learned to think like an archaeologist. I was in high school when I started working there. In the three summers I was involved in the excavation I learned how to look at culture from the dirt up. It was a remarkable pleasure that I was able to 'return' to St. John's some thirty years later to help develop the exhibit and tell the many stories this site holds," said Silas Hurry.

Maintaining St. John's site and the museum is an ongoing project. During the course of excavations that spanned decades, Garry Stone, Henry Miller, Ruth Mitchell, and other archaeologists deliberately left certain areas of the site unexcavated. Those areas are, in a sense, a contract between today's archaeologists and scientists of the future. Tomorrow's scientists will revisit the site with technologies that today's archaeologists can only imagine. They will reveal archaeological ghosts still hiding at St. John's—and Miller is sure there are plenty of them. Future historians will find documents yet undiscovered in an archive, an old house, a museum, or a library. Miller is certain they are there too.

"Inside St. John's walls people endeavored to build a new society, one where people of different beliefs and backgrounds could live together peacefully," Miller said. "It's a place where important things happened, things that shaped life in America. The issues they struggled with—the place of faith in government, liberty of conscience for individuals, the roles of men and women, incorporating immigrants, using the environment, property rights, finding opportunity—continue today and have to be addressed anew by the latest generation. Excavating this site, meeting these people, provoked a thrill of discovery and passion for exploring the past that has inspired me down to this day," Miller added.

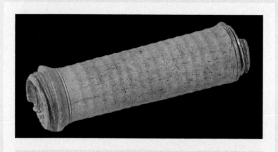

Mysteries still remain at St. John's. Originally, archaeologists thought this artifact made of bone was part of a musical instrument. Then they thought it might be a needle case. However, a similar object, recently found elsewhere, suggests it may have been part of a telescope or even a microscope.

In addition to the human connections, St. John's perfectly shows how the historical and archaeological records complement each other; how together history and science create a vivid picture of past lives. During ten seasons of excavation at St. John's, the archaeologists produced many records and images as part of the archaeological record of excavation. Historians and scientists have already learned a lot from 1.5 million artifacts removed from the site, but more information may yet be teased out. And many stories still remain buried in the soil and in archives. New analysis methods and determined digging by future archaeologists and historians will find these tales and reveal more information about St. John's and its residents.

The continuing story of St. John's house is amazing. But it's not the only amazing place in American history. Every town in this country has its own ghost walls that once surrounded people who lived and worked inside them. When archaeologists scrape away the soil that buries them or when historians open the doors of archives, those ghost walls are ready to share their stories. And even as we learn about them from their tales, we may discover that we are also learning something new about ourselves.

Evoking the spirit of its seventeenth-century ancestor,
St. John's museum invites visitors to enter and explore.

AUTHOR'S NOTE

St. John's house and I first met in 2005, while I was at St. Mary's City doing research for my book *Written in Bone*. At that time, the archaeologists were uncovering the front yard and backyard features. The A-frame surrounded the cobblestone foundation, and the museum was still a paper dream. My storyteller's instincts went on high alert when Henry Miller told me about some of the people who had lived in the house and the events that had occurred there.

During my second and third visits to St. Mary's City, in 2009 and 2013, I came to know St. John's house as if it were part of my own neighborhood. I slid down the overgrown but still visible-to-those-who-look-carefully path to the freshwater stream where many servants—and maybe John Lewger Jr.— filled buckets with water. In the quiet moments just before sunset, I sat on the ground outside the museum, and thought about John and Anne Lewger, the trial concerning Edward the Indian boy, Antonio, Simon Overzee, Margaret Brent, Charles Calvert, and Wastahunda Hariguera. My imagination brought all of them back to the site. In the daytime, I walked back and forth from the house to the center of town and to the area where the first Catholic chapel most likely stood. As I stood in the chapel field—a large cemetery of unmarked colonial graves—I wondered where the remains of Anne Lewger, Leonard Calvert, and Mary Calvert lay buried. At the Godiah Spray house, a re-created tobacco plantation at St. Mary's City, I spoke with living history interpreters and used reproductions of seventeenth-century tools. I even picked a hornworm off a tobacco leaf! (Unlike colonial field laborers, I just moved it to another location.)

Silas Hurry, Ruth Mitchell, and Tim Riordan shared a wealth of information about St. John's freehold and its artifacts, St. Mary's City, and Maryland's early colonists. Garry Wheeler Stone and Wesley Willoughby spiced up the mix with tales of their discoveries. Living history interpreters Peter Friesen, John Harvey, Aaron Meisinger, Roberta Smith, and twins Carter and Samuel Harris described the ins and outs of seventeenth-century colonists' daily lives. Genie Posnett and Debra Watson showed me reproductions of period clothing—and explained how they were worn. I collected at least three books' worth of fascinating information. Regretfully, I couldn't use everything. But I loved hearing every minute of it. Susan Wilkinson and Don Winter, also at St. Mary's City, helped me locate wonderful photographic images. In 2005 Lois Green Carr shared her research into the Calvert family and colonial Maryland with me.

On a "Maryland Roots" trip to England, Henry Miller took my husband and me to visit Kiplin Hall, George Calvert's country estate, and Hook House, Cecil and Anne Arundell Calvert's home. Kiplin Hall is a magnificent, grand estate, but Cecil and Anne's much smaller home stole my heart. Perhaps more than any place I've been, I could feel history in that house, still lived in by Arundell descendants. The sculpted plaster reliefs of the *Ark* and the *Dove* on the sitting room ceiling helped me realize more about what mattered to Cecil Calvert. In London we visited St. Giles in the Fields cemetery, where John Lewger, a victim of the 1665 plague, and Cecil Calvert are buried.

The staff at the Maryland State Archives and the Maryland Historical Society helped me locate many primary source documents. Deciphering seventeenth-century handwriting is definitely a time-consuming labor of love, but it's more than worth the effort. Quotes from these documents enabled me to tell the colonists' stories with their own words.

Above all, I couldn't have told this ghost story without the help of Henry Miller. He patiently answered hundreds of questions that I asked as we trudged through the woods at St. John's, walked the chapel field at St. Mary's City and country lanes in England, looked at artifacts in the laboratory, and ate in various restaurants and pubs. (Authors do eat.) He answered follow-up questions via e-mail or on the telephone, all with good cheer. I owe Henry paragraphs of heartfelt thanks for enriching not only my research horizons but for leading my husband and me on adventures that are now often-told stories in the Walker family oral tradition.

TIMELINE

1632 George Calvert dies, and Cecil Calvert receives the royal charter granting him the colony of Maryland.

March 1634 The *Ark* and *Dove* arrive in Maryland and colonists establish St. Mary's City as the colony's capital city.

November 28, 1637 John Lewger, the first provincial secretary of the colony of Maryland, his family, and seven servants arrive in St. Mary's City.

Spring 1638 Construction begins on St. John's house, the Lewgers' home.

March 23, 1642 Mathias de Sousa, formerly an indentured servant, becomes the first person of African ancestry to serve and vote in an American legislature.

1645 Ingle's Rebellion begins, and the Maryland colony is attacked.

June 9, 1647 Leonard Calvert dies.

January 21, 1648 Margaret Brent asks to have two votes in the Maryland General Assembly.

1650 John Lewger Jr. sells St. John's house and freehold to Henry Fox.

1654 Henry Fox sells St. John's to Simon Overzee.

September 1656	Antonio, an enslaved African, dies at St. John's.
1660	Simon Overzee dies.
September 1661	St. John's becomes the home of Charles Calvert, son of Cecil Calvert.
June 1666	Susquehannock war chiefs Wastahunda Hariguera and Gosweinquerackqua sign a peace treaty at St. John's.
1666–1695	St. John's house serves as a public inn operated by various innkeepers, including Henry Exon.
1695	Maryland's capital and governmental seat relocates to Annapolis.
circa 1720	St. John's house and its outbuildings become ruins buried beneath agricultural fields.
1962	Henry Chandlee Forman conducts archaeological investigations at St. John's house.
1972–1976	St. John's Freehold becomes the first seventeenth-century site in Maryland to be intensively excavated using the principles of scientific archaeology.
2002–2005	Additional archaeological excavations are conducted at St. John's.
2008	Construction of St. John's museum is completed and opens to the public in September.

SOURCE NOTES

4   *Archives of Maryland*, 41:190–191, accessed April 1, 2014, http://msa.maryland.gov/megafile/msa/speccol/sc2900/sc2908/html/index.html.

10 Silas Hurry, personal communication to the author, December 4, 2013.

12 Clayton Colman Hall, ed., *Narratives of Early Maryland 1633–1684* (New York: Charles Scribner's Sons, 1910), 344.

16–17 Ibid., 16.

17 *The Calvert Papers*, 3:20–21, accessed April 1, 2014, http://memory.loc.gov/cgi-bin/query/h?ammem/lhbcbbib:@field%28NUMBER+@band%28lhbcb+3364a%29%29.

17 Hall, *Narratives of Early Maryland*, 41.

17 *Calvert Papers*, 3:21.

18 Hall, *Narratives of Early Maryland*, 16.

19 Ibid., 91.

20 Ibid., 79.

22 Henry Miller, personal communicaiton to the author, April 13, 2013.

25 Silas Hurry, personal communication to the author, April 12, 2013.

25 Henry Miller, personal communication to the author, February 4, 2013.

26, 28 Henry Miller, personal communication to the author, April 12, 2013.

28–29 Ibid.

29 Henry Miller, personal communication to the author, April 10, 2013.

34 Henry Miller, personal communication to the author, November 29, 2013.

36 Henry Miller, personal communication to the author, May 1, 2013.

38–39 Henry Miller, personal communication to the author, February 4, 2013.

47 Garry Wheeler Stone, *Society, Housing, and Architecture in Early Maryland: John Lewger's St. John's*, University of Pennsylvania PhD dissertation, 1982 (Ann Arbor, MI: University Microfilms International, 1990), 37.

47 Silas Hurry, personal communication to the author, April 9, 2013.

48 Henry Miller, personal communication to the author, April 1, 2013.

49 Ibid.

50 Stone, *Society, Housing, and Architecture*, 133.

51–52 Henry Miller, personal communication to the author, July 22, 2013.

52 *Archives of Maryland*, 4:189.

52–53 Henry Miller, personal communication to the author, July 22, 2013.

55 *Archives of Maryland*, 4:196.

56 *Calvert Papers*, 1:199.

57 Henry Miller, personal communication to the author, April 10, 2013.

66–68 Henry Miller, personal communication to the author, January 7, 2014.

69 Silas Hurry, personal communication to the author, August 15, 2013.

69   Henry Miller, personal communication to the author, May 21, 2013.

72   *Archives of Maryland*, 1:33.

72–74 *Archives of Maryland*, 4:180.

75   *Archives of Maryland*, 3:187.

75   *Calvert Papers*, 1:198.

76   Ibid.

76   *Archives of Maryland*, 4:277.

78   Henry Miller, personal communication to the author, May 22, 2014.

79   Henry Miller, personal communication to the author, June 5, 2013.

81   Edwin W. Beitzell, "Tomas Cornwallis (Cornwaleys), Plaintiff vs. Richard Ingle, Defendant: Testimony of John Lewger and Cuthbert Fenwick 1645–1646," *Chronicles of St. Mary's* 26, no. 2 (1978): 4.

82   *Archives of Maryland*, 4:314.

83   Henry Miller, personal communication to the author, August 9, 2013.

84   *Archives of Maryland*, 1:239.

85   *Archives of Maryland*, 10:365.

86   *Archives of Maryland*, 41:42.

88   Henry Miller, personal communication to the author, August 6, 2013.

88   Ibid.

89   Wesley Willoughby, personal communication to the author, June 10, 2013.

89   Silas Hurry, personal communication to the author, December 4, 2013.

89   Wesley Willoughby, personal communication to the author, June 10, 2013.

90   Henry Miller, personal communication to the author, April 4, 2013.

90   Henry Miller, personal communication to the author, August 6, 2013.

91   *Archives of Maryland*, 4:190.

91   Henry Miller, personal communication to the author, July 22, 2013.

93   New York State Archives, New York (Colony), Council, series A1810-78, 12:11.

93   B. Fernow, ed., *Documents Relating to the History of the Dutch and Swedish Settlements on the Delaware River*, vol. XII (Albany, NY: Argus, 1877), 93–94.

93   *Archives of Maryland*, 41:190–191, 204–206.

93   *Archives of Maryland*, 1:533–534.

93   *Archives of Maryland*, 41:205.

95   Ibid., 190.

97   Ibid., 211.

97   Ibid., 255.

102   *Calvert Papers*, 1:268.

102   Ibid., 229.

102   Garry Wheeler Stone, e-mail to the author, August 4, 2013.

103   Robert Winston Keeler, "The Homelot on the Seventeenth-Century Chesapeake Tidewater Frontier," PhD dissertation, University of Oregon, September 1977, 44.

103   *Calvert Papers*, 1:244.

103   Ibid., 246.

104	Henry Miller, personal communication to the author, August 6, 2013.
105	Henry Miller, personal communication to the author, August 5, 2013.
105	Henry Miller, personal communication to the author, August 6, 2013.
105	Keeler, "The Homelot on the Seventeenth-Century Chesapeake Tidewater Frontier," 44.
105–106	Henry Miller, personal communication to the author, August 6, 2013.
106	*Calvert Papers*, 1:246.
107	*Archives of Maryland*, 3:549.
107	*Archives of Maryland*, 2:136.
107	Ibid., 15.
107	*Archives of Maryland*, 3:549.
108	Ibid., 549–550.
108	Henry Miller, personal communication to the author, August 7, 2013.
108	*Archives of Maryland*, 15:57.
109	*Archives of Maryland*, 2:454.
111	Henry Miller, personal communication to the author, May 3, 2013.
116	Henry Miller, personal communication to the author, August 1, 2013.
117	Henry Miller, personal communication to the author, January 10, 2014.
118–119	Henry Miller, personal communication to the author, June 5, 2013.
119	Ruth Mitchell, personal communication to the author, December 2, 2013.
121	Ruth Mitchell, personal communication to the author, June 4, 2013.
121–122	Ruth Mitchell, personal communication to the author, December 2, 2013.
123	Henry Miller, personal communication to the author, December 3, 2013.
124	Silas Hurry, personal communication to the author, December 3, 2013.
124–125	Henry Miller, personal communication to the author, December 3, 2013.

SELECTED BIBLIOGRAPHY

Beitzell, Edwin W. "Tomas Cornwallis (Cornwaleys), Plaintiff vs. Richard Ingle, Defendant: Testimony of John Lewger and Cuthbert Fenwick 1645–1646." *Chronicles of St. Mary's 26*, no. 2 (1978), 1–8.

Bernard, L. Leon. "Some New Light on the Early Years of the Baltimore Plantation." *Maryland Historical Magazine* XLIV, no. 2 (June 1949): 93–100.

Blanton, Dennis, and Julia A. King, eds. *Indian and European Contact in Context: The Mid-Atlantic Region*. Gainesville: University Press of Florida, 2004.

Carr, Lois Green. "Adaptation and Settlement in the Colonial Chesapeake." *St. Mary's City Research Series No. 6*. Historic St. Mary's City: Alexander H. Morrison Fund Publication, 1987.

Carr, Lois Green, Russell R. Menard, and Lorena S. Walsh. *Robert Cole's World*. Chapel Hill: University of North Carolina Press, 1991.

Carr, Lois Green, Philip D. Morgan, and Jean B. Russo. *Colonial Chesapeake Society.* Chapel Hill: University of North Carolina Press, 1998.

Carr, Lois Green, and Lorena S. Walsh. "The Planter's Wife: The Experience of White Women in Seventeenth-Century Maryland." *William and Mary Quarterly*, 3rd ser., 34, no. 4 (October 1977): 542–571.

Clark, Alice. *Working Life of Women in the Seventeenth Century.* New York: Harcourt, 1920.

Fernow, B., ed. *Documents Relating to the History of the Dutch and Swedish Settlements on the Delaware River.* Vol. XII. Albany, NY: Argus, 1877. Accessed online March 7, 2013. http://archive.org/details/documentsrelativ12brod.

Forman, Henry Chandlee. *Jamestown and St. Mary's: Buried Cities of Romance.* Baltimore: Johns Hopkins Press, 1938.

Foster, James W. "George Calvert: His Yorkshire Boyhood." *Maryland Historical Magazine* 55, no. 4 (December 1960): 261–273.

Gibb, James G., and Julia A. King. "Gender, Activity Areas, and Homelots in the 17th-Century Chesapeake Region." *Historical Archaeology* 25, no. 4 (1991): 109–131.

Hall, Clayton Colman, ed. *Narratives of Early Maryland 1633–1684.* New York: Charles Scribner's Sons, 1910.

Harrington, J. C. "Dating Stem Fragments of Seventeenth and Eighteenth Century Clay Tobacco Pipes." *Quarterly Bulletin of the Archaeological Society of Virginia* 9, no.1 (September 1954): 9–13.

Heywood, Linda M., and John K. Thornton. *Central Africans, Atlantic Creoles, and the Foundation of the Americas, 1585–1660.* New York: Cambridge University Press, 2007.

Jordan, David W. *Foundations of Representative Government in Maryland, 1632–1715.* Cambridge: Cambridge University Press, 1987.

Keeler, Robert Winston. *The Homelot on the Seventeenth-Century Chesapeake Tidewater Frontier.* PhD dissertation, University of Oregon, 1977.

Krugler, John D. *English and Catholic: The Lords Baltimore in the Seventeenth Century.* Baltimore: Johns Hopkins University Press, 2004.

Main, Gloria L. *Tobacco Colony: Life in Early Maryland, 1650–1720.* Princeton, NJ: Princeton University Press, 1983.

Middleton, Arthur Pierce, and Henry M. Miller. "John Lewgar and the St. John's Site: The Story of Their Role in Creating the Colony of Maryland." *Maryland Historical Magazine* 103, no. 2 (2008): 132–165.

Phung, Thao T., Julia A. King, and Douglas H. Ubelaker. "Alcohol, Tobacco, and Excessive Animal Protein: The Question of an Adequate Diet in the Seventeenth-Century Chesapeake." *Historical Archaeology* 43, no. 2 (2009): 61–82.

Riordan, Timothy B. *The Plundering Time: Maryland and the English Civil War, 1645–1646.* Baltimore: Maryland Historical Society, 2004.

Russo, Jean B., and J. Elliott Russo. *Planting an Empire: The Early Chesapeake in British North America.* Baltimore: Johns Hopkins University Press, 2012.

Semmes, Raphael. *Crime and Punishment in Early Maryland.* Montclair, NJ: Patterson Smith, 1966.

Steiner, Bernard Christian, ed. *Archives of Maryland. Proceedings of the Provincial Court of Maryland 1658–1662*. Vol. 41. Baltimore: Maryland Historical Society, 1922.

Stone, Garry Wheeler. "The Roof Leaked, but the Price Was Right: The Virginia House Reconsidered." *Maryland Historical Magazine*, no. 3 (Fall 2004): 313–328.

———. *Society, Housing, and Architecture in Early Maryland: John Lewger's St. John's*. University of Pennsylvania PhD dissertation, 1982. Ann Arbor, MI: University Microfilms International, 1990.

———. "St. John's: Archaeological Questions and Answers." *Maryland Historical Magazine* 69, no. 2 (Summer 1974): 146–168.

Thornton, John. *Africa and Africans in the Making of the Atlantic World, 1400–1800*. New York: Cambridge University Press, 1998.

Walsh, Lorena S. *Motives of Honor, Pleasure, and Profit: Plantation Management in the Colonial Chesapeake, 1607–1763*. Chapel Hill: University of North Carolina Press, 2010.

Walsh, Lorena S., and Russell R. Menard. "Death in the Chesapeake: Two Life Tables for Men in Early Colonial Maryland." *Maryland Historical Magazine* 69:211–227.

White, Andrew. *A Relation of Maryland*. March of America Facsimile series, no. 22. Ann Arbor, MI: University Microfilms, 1966.

FURTHER READING

Day, Nancy. *Your Travel Guide to Colonial America*. Minneapolis: Twenty-First Century Books, 2001.

Huie, Lois Miner. *Ick! Yuck! Eew! Our Gross American History*. Minneapolis: Millbrook Press, 2014.

Maestro, Betsy. *The New Americans: Colonial Times: 1620–1689*. New York: Harper Collins, 2004.

Miller, Brandon Marie. *Dressed for the Occasion: What Americans Wore, 1620–1970*. Minneapolis: Twenty-First Century Books, 1999.

———. *Good Women of a Well-Blessed Land: Women's Lives in Colonial America*. Minneapolis: Twenty-First Century Books, 2003.

Walker, Sally M. *Written in Bone: Buried Lives of Jamestown and Colonial Maryland*. Minnepaolis: Carolrhoda Books, 2009.

For more information about Historic St. Mary's City, its inhabitants, and ongoing archaeology, see the Historic St. Mary's City website: https://www.hsmcdigshistory. org/.

For information about the archaeology at another Chesapeake Bay seventeenth-century site, see the Jamestown Rediscovery website: http://www.apva.org/jr.html.

LERNER

SOURCE

Expand learning beyond the printed book. Download free, complementary educational resources for this book from our website, www.lerneresource.com.

INDEX

ABOUT THE AUTHOR

Sally M. Walker is the author of many award-winning books for young readers. Her *Secrets of a Civil War Submarine: Solving the Mysteries of the* H. L. Hunley won the Association for Library Service to Children's prestigious Robert F. Sibert Informational Book Medal in 2006. She is also the author of *Written in Bone: Buried Lives of Jamestown and Colonial Maryland, Their Skeletons Speak: Kennewick Man and the Paleoamerican World,* and *Boundaries: How the Mason-Dixon Line Settled a Family Feud and Divided a Nation.* When she isn't busy writing or doing research for books, Ms. Walker works as a children's literature consultant. She lives in DeKalb, Illinois. Visit her online at www.sallymwalker.com.

PHOTO ACKNOWLEDGMENTS

The images in this book are used with the permission of: Images courtesy of Historic St. Mary's City, pp. 1, 3, 7, 8 (all), 9, 10 (all), 11 (all), 15 (bottom), 18, 19, 24, 27, 28 (top), 30, 31 (bottom left, bottom right), 32, 33 (all), 34 (all), 35 (all), 37 (bottom), 39 (top), 42, 43 (all), 45 (bottom left), 46 (bottom), 47, 48 (all), 49 (all), 51 (all), 53, 57, 58 (bottom), 59 (bottom), 60, 61, 62 (all), 63, 64 (top left, top right, middle), 65, 67, 68, 69, 70 (all), 76, 77 (all), 79, 80, 81 (all), 87 (right), 89, 96 (all), 101 (all), 103, 105 (all), 109 (bottom), 110 (all), 112 (top), 113, 114, 120 (all), 121, 122, 123, 124, 125; The Walters Art Museum, p. 13 (left); © Sally Walker, pp.13 (right), 16 (all), 17, 45 (top, bottom right), 46 (top), 58 (top), 59 (top), 66; Maryland State Archives, pp. 14 (MSA SC 1399-1-526), 52 (Land Office, Patent Record, Original, 1646–1657, liber ABH, folio 65, MSA S920-4, 1/29/2/45), 55 (General Assembly Upper House proceedings 1637–1658, Liber MC, folio 178, MSA S-977-1, 2/20/4/42); Cecil Calvert, by William Wirtz after Florence McCubbin after Gerard Soest. Courtesy of Historic St. Mary's City, p. 15 (top); Images courtesy of Historic St. Mary's City. L.H.Barker © 2009. All rights reserved, pp. 21, 54, 90, 92, 104, 115; © Laura Westlund/Independent Picture Service, pp. 26, 31 (top); Images courtesy of Historic St. Mary's City. L.H.Barker © 2007. All rights reserved, pp. 28 (bottom), 37 (top), 41 (all), 74, 98, 109 (top), 112 (bottom); Courtesy of Jefferson Patterson Park and Museum. William Henry Holmes, "Aboriginal Pottery of the Eastern United States," 1903, Fig. CXXXVII, p. 39 (bottom); Courtesy, Winterthur Museum, Knife, maker: Sanderson, 1800–1875, Sheffield, England, Iron, Bone, bequest of Henry Francis du Pont, 1965.2280.001,.002, p. 64 (bottom); Detail, Photograph by Chip Clark, Smithsonian Institution, p. 73; Courtesy, Ceramics in America; photo, Gavin Ashworth, p. 87 left; New York State Archives. New York (Colony). Council. Dutch colonial administrative correspondence, 1646–1664. Series A1810-78. Volume 12, page 11, p. 94; Charles Calvert by Ada Cole Chase after Peter Lely. Courtesy of Historic St. Mary's City, p. 100; Image courtesy of Historic St. Mary's City/original Maryland Archives, p. 108.
Cover images: © Don Winter/Historic St. Mary's City.